CO ARF-220

TENNIS:
A Guide For The
Developing Tennis Player

James E. Bryant, Ed.D.

Metropolitan State College, Denver

Morton Publishing Company
295 W. Hampden, Suite 104
Englewood, Colorado 80110

GV
995
·B790
C. 2

Copyright © 1984 by Morton Publishing Company

All rights reserved. No part of this publication may be reproduced, stored in a
retrieval system, or transmitted, in any form or by any means, electronic,
mechanical, photocopying, recording, or otherwise, without the prior written
permission of the publisher.

Printed in the United States of America

ISBN: 0-89582-101-X

H 609566   BL

Table of Contents

Acknowledgments i
Preface iii
Chapter One — Preliminaries to the Strokes in Tennis:
    An Introduction 1
Chapter Two — Groundstrokes 13
Chapter Three — The Volley............................. 43
Chapter Four — The Service and Service Return............ 51
Chapter Five — The Lob and Overhead
    Smash Combination....................... 69
Chapter Six — Other Strokes to be Aware
    Of and Recognize 81
Chapter Seven — Putting the Strokes Together
    With Agility 87
Chapter Eight — Physical Aspects to Playing Tennis 91
Chapter Nine — Etiquette and Rules Interpretation 99
Chapter Ten — Singles Strategy............................ 109
Chapter Eleven — Doubles Strategy 123
Chapter Twelve — Drills for the Developing Player 137
Chapter Thirteen — Mental Aspects
    of Tennis Competition 149
Chapter Fourteen — The Court and the Equipment 157
Chapter Fifteen — Resources in Tennis 163
Chapter Sixteen — The Roots of Tennis 169
Appendix — The Developing Player's
    Self-Appraisal Checklist....................... 173
Glossary of Tennis Terms 179
USTA Rules of Tennis and Cases and Decisions, 1983 183
Index 197

Acknowledgments

Several individuals have contributed to the development of this text. The efforts, concern, and contributions in executing correct tennis skills as tennis models are much appreciated from Patty Blalack, Tim Bryant, Marilyn Garrett, Lisa Moyers, and Steve Taylor. The beautiful diagrams of various strategies and drills by illustrator Darryl Wisnia add significantly to the understanding of the material in the book.

Aspen Leaf Sporting Goods is acknowleged for permitting photographs within the store, and Gates Tennis Center is acknowledged for permitting photographs to be shot on their courts.

Preface

TENNIS: A GUIDE FOR THE DEVELOPING TENNIS PLAYER is designed for beginning and intermediate tennis players. It is planned for the student actively receiving tennis instruction and as a guide for future reference.

The sixteen chapters are set up in a logical sequence of learning experiences that include: basic tennis strokes; development of a fitness level to play the game; understanding of the behavior and rules that govern play; understanding of game stratagies; practice applications for the developing player; coordination of mind and body into the mental aspects of play; and learning about court surfaces and equipment, additional resources related to tennis, and the background of tennis. Each chapter will assist the reader in understanding the game of tennis in a simplistic and clear manner. Photographs and diagrams provide visual samples of strokes, strategy, and basic concepts. Sections related to skill acquisition are reinforced with capsule learning experience suggestions, and with an "elimination of errors" review to facilitate an indepth understanding of those skills.

Tennis is a highly popular sport played at all levels of skill and by all ages. It requires a strong foundation of skill, an indepth comprehension of the intricacy of the flow of the game, and an insight into the rules of play. It is a game that is played at an intense level of competition by some and in a spirit of enjoyment by all who understand that tennis is a game. Tennis, as played today, is a never-ending learning experience for the player. It is a complex game that, when played and practiced over the years, becomes surprisingly simplistic and yet always remains challenging.

This material is truly a guide for the developing tennis player who is taking instruction through courses or lessons, and who will continue to grow with the game through the years.

Chapter One

Preliminaries to The Strokes in Tennis

AN INTRODUCTION

To play tennis, it is imperative to know how to hold a tennis racket for a particular stroke, and how to stand and move. Recognizing the spin of the ball, although not of immediate concern to the beginner, is extremely important as the player's skills develop. It is also wise to gain a comprehension of racket face control and have a feel for the ball as the racket impacts the ball. Learning how to grip and control a tennis racket, and how to get ready to hit the ball, are skills that must be established early in the learning experience.

BASIC TENNIS GRIPS

The use of a tennis grip when hitting a particular stroke is directly related to the execution of that stroke. The selection of a tennis grip that fits the stroke is necessary to complete the stroke with acceptable form.

The *eastern forehand grip*, a universally used grip designed for executing the forehand groundstroke, is also called the "shake hands" grip. Place your racket hand on the strings of the racket, and bring your hands straight down to the grip. As your hand grasps the racket grip, your fingers will be spread along the length of the racket grip with the index finger spread the furthest in a "trigger finger" style, providing control. The thumb will be situated on the back side of the racket, and a "V" will be formed by the thumb and the four fingers on the racket grip. The "V" points to the racket shoulder when the racket is held in front of the player at a right angle to the body.

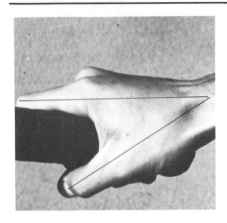

Eastern Forehand Grip Top   *Eastern Forehand Side*

The *eastern backhand grip* is a conventional backhand grip used extensively in tennis. From the eastern forehand grip, roll your hand over the top of the racket grip and place your thumb diagonally across the rear plane of the racket grip. You should be able to see all four knuckles of the racket hand from this position when the racket is held perpendicular to the body. The "V" formed by the thumb and fingers will point to the non-racket shoulder when the racket is held in front of the body.

Eastern Backhand Top   *Eastern Backhand Side*

The *continental forehand grip* and *continental backhand grip* are essentially the same. They differ from the eastern forehand and backhand grips in that the hand is placed midway between the positioning of the two eastern grips. The "V" formed by the thumb and fingers points to the middle or center of the body halfway between the racket and non-racket sides of the body when the racket is held in front of the body. The subtle difference between the forehand and backhand placement of the hands for the continental grip is that, in the forehand grip, the thumb grasps the racket grip, whereas in the backhand, the thumb is placed diagonally across the rear of the racket grip.

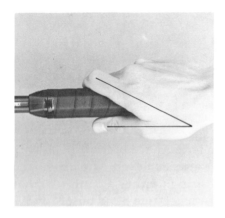

Forehand-Backhand
Continental Grip Top

Forehand-Backhand
Continental Grip Side

Thumb Position Forehand
Continental Grip Side

Thumb Position Backhand
Continental Grip Side

The *western forehand grip* is often used by those who have received no instruction in tennis, or it is used for special strokes. The grip is best achieved by laying the racket on the court and picking it up naturally. The palm of the hand faces flat against and under the back side of the racket grip. The "V" formed by the thumb and fingers, when the racket is held in front of the body, points beyond the racket shoulder.

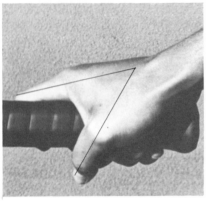

Western Forehand Grip Top

Western Forehand Grip Side

The use of the two-hand grips in tennis have become popular in recent years. The *two-hand backhand grip* is achieved when the hand on the racket side grasps the racket grip in either a continental or eastern backhand grip, with the non-racket-side hand butted above that grasp in an eastern forehand grip. The two-hand backhand grip must be a snug fit of two hands working together to execute the stroke. There is also a two-hand forehand grip that is used by a few players, but the grip is not widely used at this time.

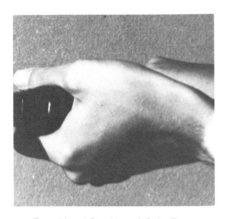

Two-Hand Backhand Grip Top

Two-Hand Backhand Grip Side

The selection of the grip is based on a particular purpose. Eastern forehand grips are used for the forehand groundstroke and for flat serves, while the eastern backhand grip is used for the backhand groundstroke and for special serves. The continental grips are used for groundstrokes, net play, and for the slice and topspin serves. The continental grip has the added advantage of requiring little in the way of grip adjustment for different strokes; consequently, strokes are disguised when this grip is used. The western forehand is used with success when hitting topspin forehand groundstrokes. Both the two-hand forehand and backhand are useful grips, particularly with individuals who lack the strength to hit with more conventional grips or who are seeking more power and control for their groundstrokes. The disadvantage to these grips is that the player lacks reach for wide shots. The two-hand strokes are excellent for players who are willing to move and react to every ball hit to them.

From the perspective of *what grip to use for what stroke situation*, it is suggested that the eastern grips be used by a player who intends to stay at the baseline and hit groundstrokes. When serving, use the continental grip — it will provide control, accuracy, and power for an effective service. If you are a beginner, you may want to start by using the eastern forehand grip for the serve; however, you should switch to the continental as soon as possible. Going to the net to play a volley shot requires reaction and timing, which means that the grip should not be changed much for a forehand or backhand volley. It is recommended that the player maintain a continental grip for play at the net to avoid miss hitting the ball and being confused at the net.

Learning Experience Suggestions (Grip)

1. Keep the fingers spread down the racket grip with the index finger serving as a "trigger finger."
2. Be aware of the location of the "V" in relation to the racket and non-racket shoulders.
3. Grasp the racket firmly when assuming a grip.

THE ELIMINATION OF ERRORS

THE ERROR	WHAT CAUSES THE ERROR	CORRECTION OF THE ERROR
Lack of control of the racket.	Grasping the racket in a vise-like position.	Make sure that the fingers are spread along the racket grip.
Miss hitting a ball or poor execution.	Too tight of a grip.	Relax the grip. Grasp the racket firmly, not tightly.

CONTROLLING THE RACKET AND GETTING READY TO HIT

Racket control is essential to good strokes and thus to successful play. Three basic actions are taken when swinging a racket that will provide racket head control and that will consequently accomplish a stroke. The basic *swing action* is reflected in the forehand and backhand groundstrokes and the various lobs. The serve and overhead smashes are described through the *action of throwing*, while the *punch action* is used with forehand and backhand volleys. By executing each of these actions or patterns, you will eliminate all extraneous motion, which will help you to simplify the action of each stroke.

Flat Racket Face

There are also three basic *racket face* positions that affect the control and flight pattern of the ball, followed by the bounce of the ball on the surface of the court. The effect of these three racket face positions on the resultant action of the ball is dependent on the speed of the racket head hitting through the ball and on the angle of the racket face when it contacts the ball. If contact is made with the *racket face flat* to the ball, the flight of the ball will be straight, with the ball falling to the court surface due to gravity. An *open racket face* will cause the ball to have a floating action in its flight, spinning in a backward motion. A *closed racket face* will force the flight pattern of the ball downward due to the ball having a forward spin. Each racket face position is important to all skill levels of players, and understanding what causes the drop or rise of the ball gives the developing player a greater insight into the total concept of hitting the ball and reacting to the bounce.

Open Racket Face

Closed Racket Face

　　Comprehending spins is a direct carryover from understanding racket head and racket face control. A tennis shot that is hit without spin is affected by three aspects of the overall stroke. First, as the ball strikes the racket face, a direct force is applied to the ball that provides velocity and determines the flight pattern of the ball. Secondly, that velocity is countered by air resistance and gravity, with the former impeding the velocity of the tennis ball and the latter pulling the ball down toward the court. Finally, the ball will strike the tennis court surface at an angle equal to the rebound of the ball off the court surface.

　　When a ball spins in its flight pattern, the tennis player must also cope with the behavior of the ball as it strikes the court surface. There are three *basic actions for balls in flight*. First, *topspin* is caused by the action of the top surface of the ball rotating against air resistance. This creates friction on the top part of the ball, forcing the ball in a downward path. A second spinning rotation, *underspin*, is caused by the bottom of the ball meeting air resistance and forcing the ball to stay up longer than is normally found with a non-spinning ball. The final spin action of a ball — *sidespin* — is created when the side of the ball meets air resistance and pressure. This causes the ball to veer to the opposite side.

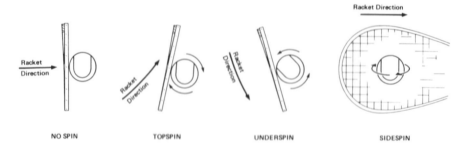

| NO SPIN | TOPSPIN | UNDERSPIN | SIDESPIN |

Basic Actions for Balls in Flight

　　The *action of the ball striking the court surface* is the end result of racket control action on the ball and the spin of the flight of the ball. As the tennis ball makes contact with the tennis court, the ball will behave in a highly predictable manner. A *topspin action* will hit the court surface with a high, deep bounce due to the forward rotation of the ball. A ball hit with *underspin* is usually hit with power and at a low angle, thus creating a skidding action as ball meets surface. The *sidespin* strikes the court with the same action and direction as the sidespin on the ball.

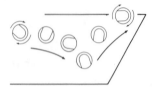

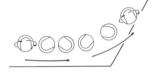

Action of Ball Striking
Court — Topspin

Action of Ball Striking
Court — Underspin

Action of Ball Striking
Court — Sidespin

In summary, there is a cause-effect relationship to racket control and spin of the ball. A flat racket face at contact will cause a flat flight pattern and flat equal angle bounce off the court. An open racket face will result in underspin during the flight of the ball and a skidding action upon contact with the court surface. A closed racket face will provide a topspin ball action with a resulting high and deep bounce off the court surface. The player should understand that there is only a subtle change in these two racket positions for the slice and topspin groundstrokes at contact. A closed racket face striking the ball on the side will create a sidespin action followed by a sideward bounce when the ball strikes the court. The developing player needs to understand the various spins applied to a ball in order to cope with balls hit with spin, and to learn how to supply spin to various strokes.

TYPES OF STROKES

As an introduction to the preliminaries of the strokes in tennis, a definition of the *various strokes* should aid in a more complete understanding of the basic skills of the game.

The basic *forehand groundstroke* is a stroke hit from the baseline following the bounce of the ball. The stroke is executed with a swinging action that produces a flat, no-spin (actually, a small amount of top-spin is found in

Forehand Groundstroke

Backhand Groundstroke

most flat shots) movement to the ball. The *backhand groundstroke* is played under the same conditions as the forehand groundstroke with the same ball action. Both are swinging action strokes with the forehand hit on the racket side of the body and the backhand hit on the non-racket side of the body. Both strokes are foundations for more advanced strokes, including *topspin* and *slice (underspin) groundstrokes. Approach shots*, which are an extension of groundstrokes, are characterized by a player advancing to the middle of the court to hit a ball. All *lobs* are also an extension of groundstrokes in terms of the swinging action.

Volley

The *volley* is a punching action characterized by playing the ball prior to contact with the tennis court. Both forehand and backhand volleys are usually played at the net, with *half-volleys* being an extension of a volley shot.

The fourth type of stroke is the basic *flat serve*, and it is described as a throwing action. Strokes that develop from the flat service are the slice service (sidespin), the topspin service, and an advanced stroke known as the American twist (another sidespin rotation). The *overhead smash* is a continuation of the basic flat service, with the key parts of the serve reflected in the smash.

Flat Serve

FEEL AND TIMING OF THE TENNIS BALL

The development of a *timing and feel for the tennis ball* is a prerequisite for successful tennis play. Regardless of the racket control, the spin of the ball, and various stroke fundamentals, the execution of each stroke is dependent on feeling and timing of the ball through *eye-hand coordination* and *focus*. Eye-hand coordination is based on past experiences of throwing and catching an object similar to a tennis ball in size. The swinging, throwing, and punching actions associated with tennis are fundamental to the ball games of batting, throwing, and catching that most American children played during their childhood. If you have played softball or racketball, or have engaged in activities like playing catch, the game of tennis will be easy for you compared to individuals who have not had those experiences.

The ability to *focus* is extremely important in tennis. The ability to "see" the ball and perceive the end result of the racket striking the ball will help the developing player improve rapidly. Being able to focus on the ball is based on the same past experiences as with eye-hand coordination. The recognition of the bounce of the ball in terms of height, the distance the ball is in relation to the player, and the relationship of the ball to the body are part of the focus concept. Additional focus points include moving to the ball, transferring weight into the ball at contact, and being in the correct position at the correct time. A final consideration is the ability to block all outside distractions and focus on the tennis ball as the only target.

*Ready Position
For a Groundstroke*

The foundation for timing and feel of the ball rests with establishing a *ready position* from which to hit groundstrokes and volleys. The ready position is the first actual skill presented for the developing player, and it is the foundation for all strokes.

The feet should be spaced slightly wider than shoulder width and should be parallel to each other. The knees are slightly bent, and the weight of the body is centered over the balls of the feet. The buttocks should be "down," with the upper body leaning slightly forward in a straight alignment. The head should be "up," looking toward the ball on the opposite side of the net. The racket is held "up" with a forehand grip on the handle, with the non-racket hand lightly touching the throat of the racket. The racket head is above the hands, and the elbows are clear of the body. The ready position gives the player the opportunity to move equally to the right or left, as well as advance forward or retreat backward. The first response from a player in

*Ready Position
Turn of Shoulders*

the ready position is to immediately rotate the shoulders when the direction of the ball from across the net is recognized. A player with good mobility will be able to move the feet quickly from the ready position. If a player can be relaxed in a ready position, keep the weight on the balls of the feet, and then react to the approaching ball with an early turn of the shoulders and quick foot movement, the stroke has been initiated positively.

Learning Experience Suggestions (Ready Position)

1. Maintain a wide base with the feet shoulder width apart.
2. Focus on the ball on the other side of the net.
3. Keep the knees slightly bent and the weight on the balls of the feet.
4. Be relaxed and ready to react.
5. Turn the shoulder early and move the feet.

THE ELIMINATION OF ERRORS

THE ERROR	WHAT CAUSES THE ERROR	CORRECTION OF THE ERROR
Falling off balance.	Feet too close together.	Widen the base.
Miss timing the ball.	Not focusing on the ball and not getting shoulders rotated early with feet moving.	Watch the seams of the ball, and rotate the shoulders early. Also, move the feet.

Chapter Two

Groundstrokes

Groundstrokes are crucial to success in tennis, and they are executed by the player hitting the tennis ball from the baseline area following one bounce of the ball on the court. The groundstroke involves a swinging action designed to hit the ball deep to the opponent's baseline. Both forehand and backhand groundstrokes develop from the basic (little spin) flat stroke and evolve into topspin and slice (underspin) groundstrokes. The two-hand forehand and backhand also originate from the basic flat groundstroke, with alterations giving the two-hand groundstrokes their own identity. To accomplish the groundstroke, get in the ready position, and then decide whether to use the forehand or backhand.

GROUNDSTROKES — BASIC FOREHAND

The *basic forehand groundstroke* is the foundation for all forehands hit with spin, and it is the stroke most used by players if they are given the choice of which stroke to use.

The eastern forehand grip — also known as the "shake hands," grip (see Chapter 1) — is used to execute the basic forehand groundstroke.

The basic forehand groundstroke involves three stages — preparing to hit the ball, contacting the ball, and following through. Each stage must be performed in sequence.

Preparing to hit the ball begins with the player in the ready position. Two reactions follow: 1) rotation of the shoulders and 2) movement of the feet. The racket has to be placed in an early backswing position as a result of the shoulder and foot movement. To do this, the player may either bring the racket straight back or loop the racket. Either is acceptable, since the goal is to get the racket back in a low position to hit from a semi-low to high position. The loop will be emphasized in this situation as the best method to get the racket back early and in proper position.

Forehand Groundstroke Loop Sequence

The *loop* is broken into two sections: 1) pulling the racket back in a line even with the eye, and 2) dropping the racket below the line of the ball at about a twelve-inch position below and behind the intended impact area of the ball.

The loop will provide a rhythm to the swing, add extra velocity to the ball following impact, and insure a grooved swing.

The full pattern for this *preparation* is to bring the racket back as quickly as possible by reacting early to the ball, and turn the shoulders to begin inertia. As the racket starts back in the loop following the shoulder turn, both feet will move and pivot automatically to accommodate the upper body turn. The racket should move to a perpendicular position to the fence beyond the back court, with the racket slightly higher than the hand and the wrist in a firm position. The arm should be firm, with the elbow slightly bent and away from the body. At the extreme of the backswing position the racket face and the palm will be turned slightly down to the court surface. The final part of the preparation is bending the leg.

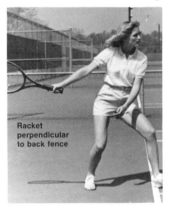

Forehand Groundstroke Preparation

Contact with the ball begins when the racket moves from the backswing in a semi-low to high pattern. The lead leg steps into the ball with a transfer of weight from back foot to lead foot. The lead leg is bent at contact while the back leg is beginning to straighten. The palm of the hand grasping the racket is behind the ball at impact, with a very firm wrist and with the arm extended eight to ten inches from the body. The non-racket arm is extended toward the ball, giving direction to the ball and balance to the body. The ball is hit off the lead leg at slightly above mid-thigh to waist level. Always step into the ball, transferring your weight forward and keeping the ball away from the body at a position toward the net and sideline.

Forehand Groundstroke Contact

Forehand Groundstroke Follow Through

The final part of the sequence is the *follow through*. The wrist remains firm and fixed, and the arm extends out across the body, with the inside of the upper arm touching the chin. The legs lift throughout the follow through, with the lead leg fully extended and the back leg slightly bent. The purpose of the follow through is to eliminate a premature lifting or pulling of the ball before it leaves the racket strings at contact.

The *position of the elbow and wrist* and the *transfer of weight* are crucial to the execution of the stroke. It must be emphasized that the wrist and arm remain firm but relaxed throughout the stroke. There is a tendency to lay the wrist back and to hyperextend the elbow. The wrist should not rotate, and the elbow can remain straight or slightly bent. Both should remain firm. Weight transfer provides

Forehand Groundstroke *Weight Transfer*

the needed drive behind the ball, with the center of gravity directed forward through the stroke by a stepping motion into the ball. During the weight transfer, the legs must be bent with a change of degree in bend through the full stroke.

Forehand Groundstroke
Close Up of Footwork and Early Preparation

Footwork and *early preparation* are both critical to success with the forehand groundstroke. Footwork supplies the mobility and balance that will provide the base for the stroke, and it sets the stage for weight transfer and leg power. Weight has to be centered over the balls of the feet to effect ease of movement, and the pivoting and lifting actions aid throughout the stroke in placing the body in a position to hit the ball. The early preparation includes good shoulder rotation and accompanying foot pivot with a loop backswing. That early response to the opponent's shot is the base for all that follows.

The stroke must be performed in full sequence, with a fluid movement from one part to the next. Any jerky, non-grooved action will detract from the stroke. The acceptable sequence has to include a coordination of feet, legs, shoulder, arm, and wrist.

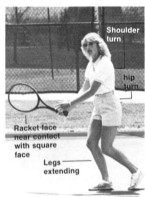

Forehand Groundstroke Sequence

Learning Experience Suggestions (Basic Forehand Groundstroke)

1. Always start from a ready position.
2. Prepare early with a shoulder rotation and pivot of the feet.
3. Activate the loop response to bring the racket back.
4. Step into the ball at contact.
5. Contact the ball with the palm-of-the-hand position.
6. Swing from slightly low to high, with the follow through extending high and across the body.
7. Keep a full synchronized sequence to the timing of the stroke.

THE ELIMINATION OF ERRORS

THE ERROR	WHAT CAUSES THE ERROR	CORRECTION OF THE ERROR
Pulling the ball to the non-racket side of the court.	Hitting too far out in front of the body or pulling the non-racket shoulder.	Step into the ball, hitting off the lead leg.
Ball directed to the near racket side of the court.	Being late in the backswing position, backswing beyond the perpendicular position to the fence, or laying the wrist too far back.	Bring back racket early with a firm wrist and a perpendicular racket backswing in relation to the fence.
Balls hit short with little velocity.	Not stepping into the ball with weight transfer, and poor racket pattern from slightly low to high.	Transfer weight into the ball at contact; change the swinging pattern to slightly low to high.
Balls hit long or high against the opponent's back fence.	Hitting the ball with poor timing, with the weight on the back foot, or in a lifting pattern at contact.	Synchronize the timing of the stroke with the slightly low to high racket pattern; use good weight transfer.

GROUNDSTROKE - TOPSPIN FOREHAND

The *topspin forehand groundstroke* is used to provide a deeply hit ball with high clearance of the net. It is an offensive weapon designed to force the opponent to play back beyond the baseline and return high-bouncing balls. It is an excellent change of pace shot, and in play at high altitude, it is the basic stroke to counteract the thin air and the effect of lack of air resistance to the ball. The ratio of success is high with a topspin forehand with the high clearance of the net and the downward rotation of the ball after it crosses the net. The view from the receiving player's position is one of a ball that clears the net by six feet or more with the exaggerated forward spin forcing the ball to arrive quickly with a sharp drop, and then a deep, high bounce. The shot is fun to hit, and it can be mastered by using a simple extension of the basic forehand stroke.

There is a subtle *change of grip* when hitting a topspin forehand if the player elects to exaggerate the topspin. The change is made by moving to a western forehand grip — a grip identified by the "V" formed by the thumb and fingers pointing between the racket shoulder and the sideline when the racket is held in front of the body. The change from an eastern to a western forehand is the player's choice. Either grip provides spin, with the western giving more spin and the eastern giving a little more control.

Again, there are three parts to hitting a successful ground-stroke, including the topspin forehand. The *preparation* requires turning the shoulder, pivoting the feet, executing the loop back-swing, and setting the racket back perpendicular to the net. As the shoulders rotate, the player may wish to change to a western grip as part of that motion. The final part of the loop brings the racket down to near foot level, with an extensive bend in the legs. The pattern of the racket head through the full stroke will be low to high. *Contact of the ball* occurs through a low to high trajectory of the racket head, with a transfer of weight to the lead foot timed to

Forehand Topspin Groundstroke Sequence

coincide with the upward motion or brush of the racket to the ball. The body is positioned away from the ball, with the ball located a step toward the net and a step toward the sideline. The non-racket arm is extended to provide balance and a reference point. The *follow through* continues the stroke with an "up" leg extension and an "up and over" arm extension. The wrist remains firm throughout the stroke, but there is a combined wrist and arm roll following contact through the end of the follow through with the racket finishing slightly horizontal.

Forehand Groundstroke Preparation
Flat versus Topspin

There are *differences between the basic forehand and the topspin forehand groundstrokes.* The grip may change from an eastern forehand to a western grip. The second portion of the loop requires a drop of the racket to the extreme back foot area, and the racket drops below the hand in the backswing position. The wrist remains firm, but the action of the wrist from the shoulder and arm rolls the racket over from contact to follow through. Finally, the low to high path is exaggerated beyond the basic forehand imparting the additional forward spin to the ball with the assistance of the

Forehand Groundstroke Contact
Flat versus Topspin

extensive knee bend at preparation to a straightening of the legs at follow through.

Forehand Groundstroke Follow Through
Flat versus Topspin

Learning Experience Suggestions (Forehand Topspin Groundstroke)

1. Drop the racket to the feet on the backswing.
2. Bend the legs low on the backswing.
3. The hitting pattern is low to high.
4. Keep the wrist firm, but roll the racket to a horizontal position on the extended follow through.
5. Change to a western grip for the full benefit of the topspin.

THE ELIMINATION OF ERRORS

THE ERROR	WHAT CAUSES THE ERROR	CORRECTION OF THE ERROR
Hitting out of the court "long" with little of the sharp drop and high bounce of the topspin.	The racket and legs are not low enough on the backswing, and/or the stroke pattern isn't low to high. Also the wrist may not be rolling over.	Get "down" on the ball and move through the stroke pattern low to high with a roll of the wrists from contact through follow through.
Trajectory of the ball over the net is only 3-4 feet.	Same as above or the grip hasn't been changed to western grip.	Same as above plus changing the grip to a more western position. Also, try dropping the racket below the hand.

GROUNDSTROKE — SLICE FOREHAND

The *slice forehand groundstroke* is used to maintain a long rally. It conserves energy, enabling the player to stay in a long rally for an extended period of time. Net clearance with a slice is low, with a skidding or low bounce of the ball following contact with the court surface. To hit the ball deep requires a low trajectory clearance of the net, since the spin action of the ball is basically underspin, which causes the ball to float. The ball doesn't have the velocity of a basic flat or topspin forehand. This gives the player more time to set up to return the shot. Players from a lower altitude use the slice to advantage by forcing a sustained rally. The same stroke at high altitude is less reliable due to the thinner air. The less air resistance permits the ball to float a longer distance, thus, reducing the consistency of the rally.

A slice forehand requires a *grip* change from eastern forehand to continental. With the racket held in front of the body, the continental grip's "V" points to the middle of the body halfway between the racket and non-racket shoulder.

The slice stroke also has three parts. The *preparation* includes the same reaction of turning the shoulders and moving the feet as the racket begins the backswing. The racket should be brought back in a straight line, with the head of the racket higher than the hand in an "up" position. As the shoulders turn, the grip should change from an eastern forehand to the continental to accommodate the need for an open-faced racket. The *contact with the ball* phase follows as the player swings from high to low, hitting off the lead leg and contacting the ball at low center. Weight transfer and bending of the legs also occur as the weight is transferred to the lead leg. The

Forehand Slice Groundstroke Sequence

non-racket arm is extended, giving a reference point and balance to the stroke. The stroke pattern is high to low to slightly high, and most balls should be hit on the rise or when the ball bounces above net height. The high-to-low pattern of follow through to contact provides a faster pace to the ball with a better chance for it staying in the court. The racket face is slightly open at contact to give the ball underspin as it travels across the net. The *follow through* is initially down, but then the racket crosses the body and ends semi-high. The forced follow through to a semi-high position insures a direction to the ball rather than a lifting. The wrist should also stay firm throughout the full stroke into the follow through.

Forehand Groundstroke Preparation Flat versus Slice

Differences between slice forehand and basic forehand include a change from the eastern forehand grip to a continental grip, which will provide a more open racket face. The loop is eliminated in favor of a straight back swing, placing the racket high and above the hand. The swing pattern is from high to low to slightly high rather than from low to high. The legs are bent, but only a small degree to give timing to the weight transfer. The ball is hit with a low trajectory and an underspin that causes a skidding reaction when

Forehand Groundstroke Contact Flat versus Slice

the ball strikes the court surface. Finally, the ball is hit on the rise or off a high bounce with the player hitting down on the ball versus hitting the ball in a low to high action.

Forehand Groundstroke Follow Through Flat versus Slice

Learning Experience Suggestions (Forehand Slice Groundstroke)

1. Bring racket high on the backswing.
2. Hit down on the ball slightly below center.
3. Follow through slightly high, maintaining an open racket face.
4. Keep the wrist firm throughout the stroke.
5. Transfer weight at contact of the ball.
6. Use a continental grip for an open face.

THE ELIMINATION OF ERRORS

THE ERROR	WHAT CAUSES THE ERROR	CORRECTION OF THE ERROR
Balls that float "long" across the baseline.	Hitting a low ball or lifting on the follow through.	Hit the ball on the rise or on the high bounce.
Hitting a ball that is short and has a large degree of backspin.	Chopping down on the ball without a slightly high follow through.	Remember to follow through slightly high and across the body.

GROUNDSTROKES — BASIC BACKHAND

The basic backhand groundstroke is the easier of the two strokes to hit (i.e., forehand vs. backhand) mechanically, yet it is the stroke that players most fail at in competition. Hitting a backhand is easy and fun, but the player must first develop confidence.

Changing Grips
For the Backhand

The *grip* used for the basic backhand is the *eastern backhand grip*, with the hand rolled onto the top of the racket grip so that the "V" is pointed to the non-racket shoulder when the racket is held in front of the body. Another guide for the grip is that the knuckles of the racket hand are aligned with the net when the racket makes contact with the ball.

As with all forehand strokes and subsequent backhands, there are three phases to the stroke that all mesh into a consistent, grooved feeling. *Preparation in hitting the ball* is based on an early reaction to the ball and on immediate rotation of both shoulders. The feet pivot during the shoulder rotation, and the racket starts its backswing movement with either the loop or straight back technique. The loop is pulled back at eye level and then dropped about eight inches below the contact point of the ball. The swinging pattern is a low-to-high action that is initiated by the backswing in preparation. A change of grips also occurs in the preparation phase. The player begins the stroke from a ready position with an eastern forehand grip. As the player reacts to the ball and turns the shoulders and pivots the feet, the racket begins its backward journey. As the racket moves back, the player uses the non-racket hand to adjust the grip by turning the racket at the throat until the top of the hand is seen as the racket follows the shoulder to the backswing position. The non-racket hand stays in contact with the throat of the racket throughout the backswing and into the movement forward to hit the ball. The racket is perpendicular to the back fence during the final extension

Backhand Groundstroke
Preparation

backward. The weight of the body is centered over the back foot and the legs are bent, permitting the body to be coiled for the next phase of the stroke.

Contact with the ball occurs with a low-to-high swinging pattern that will insure direction for the ball. The shoulder leads the elbow into the swing, and the elbow leads the wrist. This provides an accumulating effect so that at contact the racket is nearly square to the ball and the joint alignment from shoulder to wrist is a straight line. That joint alignment provides a firm base of support as the ball strikes the racket face. The weight of the body is transferred to the lead leg just prior to contact with the ball, and the position of the racket to the lead leg at contact is mid-thigh to waist level.

Backhand Groundstroke
Contact

The *follow through* is an extension of the low-to-high swinging action, with the weight continuing forward off the lead leg as the lead leg straightens and the back leg bends slightly. This provides a degree of balance to the base of the stroke. The wrist remains firm as the racket finishes high, facing the racket side of the sideline.

The *wrist, elbow, and shoulder positions* are key elements in the basic backhand groundstroke. The initial shoulder turn followed by the shoulder leading into the stroke are essential in completing the action. The elbow and the wrist should never physically be ahead of the racket. The racket should rotate around the wrist, and the wrist should rotate around the elbow from backswing to contact with the ball. At follow through, the racket should lead the wrist and elbow. If the elbow or wrist leads the racket at contact, a pushing action will result, decreasing the velocity of the ball. The racket arm stays closer to the body than with the forehand at a distance of perhaps six to eight inches.

Backhand Groundstroke
Follow Through

Racket control, weight transfer, footwork, and leg power all contribute to the success or failure of the backhand groundstroke. Racket control is characterized by the loop — pulling the racket back at eye level, then dropping the racket below the projected contact point of the ball. Balance and weight transfer occur when the player uses proper footwork from the ready position to the final follow through. The critical part of the footwork involves the singular turn of the non-racket foot when the shoulder rotates and the subsequent stepping into the ball with the racket-side foot just prior to contact with the ball. The weight transfer is a total exchange from moving weight from the back foot during preparation to the lead leg at contact on through to follow through.

Backhand Groundstroke Closeup of Wrist, Elbow, and Shoulder

　　The full sequence of actions involved in the basic backhand groundstroke will determine the outcome of the stroke. There must be a fluid sequence of movement void of all jerky or shaky movement. That sequence should include coordination of shoulders, feet, legs, elbow, and wrist into a mechanically smooth, grooved stroke that causes the racket to make contact with the ball in a nearly square position and that

Beginning of high racket head take back

Drop of racket head

Backhand Groundstroke Loop

Backhand Groundstroke Pivot to Stepping into the Ball

flows to an ultimate follow through. Combined with the mechanics of the stroke has to be the belief that the backhand is easier to execute and mechanically more sound than the forehand.

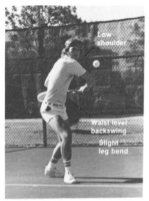

Backhand Flat Groundstroke Sequence

Learning Experience Suggestions (Basic Backhand Groundstroke)

1. Begin the stroke from the ready position.
2. Turn the shoulders early to begin the racket moving back to backswing position.
3. Use the loop backswing or a straight back motion.
4. Transfer the weight from the back foot to the front as the racket moves from backswing to contact to follow through.
5. Contact the ball slightly in front of the lead leg, with the knuckles facing the net at that contact point.
6. Swing low to high, with the racket finishing high and parallel to the racket-side sideline.
7. Change the grip from eastern forehand to eastern backhand as the racket is brought to the backswing position.
8. Keep a firm wrist, and keep the elbow and wrist behind the racket through contact.
9. Time the stroke for a full coordinated effort.

THE ELIMINATION OF ERRORS

THE ERROR	WHAT CAUSES THE ERROR	CORRECTION OF THE ERROR
Balls with no velocity that just make it across the net or hit into the net.	Elbow and/or wrist leading the racket at contact with the ball, or not changing to an eastern backhand grip.	Force the elbow and racket to stay behind the racket through contact.
Ball is hit "long" or out beyond the baseline.	Weight is still on the back foot at contact, or there is no low-to-high stroking pattern.	Transfer weight forward, and follow through on the stroke.
No control of the ball.	Too long of a backswing, not timing the contact point off the lead leg, layed back wrist, or lack of firm shoulder, arm, and wrist.	Keep the backswing perpendicular to the fence, work at good timing of the ball, or establish a firm wrist, shoulder, and arm.

GROUNDSTROKE — TOPSPIN BACKHAND

The backhand and forehand topspin groundstrokes have the common effect of providing a high trajectory, forward motion to the ball spin and a high, deep bounce to the court at contact. They are both designed for the same purpose — to keep the opponent behind the baseline and to provide a safe offensive shot. The backhand topspin is an extension of the basic backhand, and it is easy to learn and use.

Backhand Topspin Groundstroke

The *grip* for the topspin groundstroke is the *eastern backhand grip,* although some players elect to use a continental grip or two-hand backhand grip. As a reminder, the "V" of the eastern backhand grip is pointed to the non-racket shoulder when the racket is held in front of the body.

The recognizable turn of the shoulder, movement of the feet, and a loop or a straight backswing are all part of the *preparation* to hit the ball. The legs bend very low on the backswing, and the racket is positioned near the feet. As the racket moves back in the backswing, the non-racket hand adjusts the grip to an eastern backhand in preparation for the racket moving from a very low to a high position. The *contact of the ball* permits the racket to continue the trajectory of extreme low to extreme high, with the lead leg stepping into the ball to transfer the weight forward. The wrist and arm are firm throughout the stroke, but at contact the wrist and arm roll over and through the ball. The legs at contact are extending from the low preparation beginning. The *follow through* finishes high-high, with the roll of the wrist and arm bringing the

Backhand Groundstroke Preparation
Flat versus Topspin

Backhand Groundstroke Contact
Flat versus Topspin

racket face downward and across the body to the racket-side shoulder. The legs are extended at the completion of the stroke, and the weight is forward.

Differences between a topspin and a basic backhand are a lower racket head drop during the backswing (the racket is actually below the hand at its lowest position), a more pronounced bend of the knees, a more extensive low-to-high swing pattern, and a roll of the wrist through contact and follow through that forces the racket into a face-down position. All of these variations provide a high clearance of the net, a deeply hit ball with good velocity, and a high deep kick after the bounce. The backswing of the topspin backhand is lower and the racket position finishes higher than in the basic backhand.

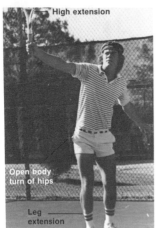

Backhand Groundstroke Follow Through Flat versus Topspin

Learning Experience Suggestions (Backhand Topspin Groundstroke)

1. Drop the racket to the feet on the backswing.

2. Bend the knees deeply and then extend through the swinging pattern.

3. The hitting pattern is extreme low to high-high.

4. Keep the wrist firm, but remember to roll the wrist and arm over the ball through contact and finish with the racket high but face-down on the follow through.

THE ELIMINATION OF ERRORS

THE ERROR	WHAT CAUSES THE ERROR	CORRECTION OF THE ERROR
Hitting long, with little of the sharp drop and high bounce.	Lack of low to very high stroke pattern, not rolling the wrist, and lack of early knee bend.	Change the stroke pattern to extreme low to high, bend the knees on the backswing with an extension at contact and follow through, and roll the wrist and arm from contact through follow through.
Lack of power and velocity transferred to the ball.	Elbow leading and poor timing.	Keep the elbow and wrist behind the racket from follow through to contact; time the contact point.
Ball hit too deep and too high beyond the baseline.	No follow through or no roll of the wrist at contact and follow through.	Follow through high with a roll of the wrist and arm.

GROUNDSTROKE - SLICE BACKHAND

The slice backhand groundstroke is a defensive stroke hit on a low trajectory with an underspin rotation. If hit with a high-to-low stroke pattern, the ball will rebound with a skid off the court surface.

The *grip* is the same conventional *eastern backhand*, but you may also use a continental or two-hand backhand grip.

Shoulder turn, foot pivot, racket coming back in a loop or straight back, and a change from an eastern forehand to an eastern backhand grip all begin the slice backhand stroke *preparation*. The racket is extended on the backswing to a high position so that a high to low to slightly high pattern can be initiated. *Contact with the ball* involves a continuing downward movement, with the racket striking the ball just below center with an open racket face. Weight is transferred forward to the lead foot, and the wrist remains firm. The *follow through* finishes with the racket head low, followed by movement of the racket across the body to the racket side shoulder in a slightly high position. The racket face will be open (to the sky). The follow through to slightly high is after the fact in terms of stroking the ball, but it is a mind set to insure proper rhythm and timing, and to eliminate carrying the ball upward off the racket, causing the ball to float.

Sequence 1

Sequence 2

Sequence 3

Sequence 4

Backhand Slice Groundstroke Sequence

The *differences observed between the slice backhand and the basic backhand* are related to the swinging action and the subsequent spin of the ball. The swing pattern of high to low to slightly high insures an underspin or slice spin as the racket makes contact below the center of the ball. If the high-to-low motion can be executed, the ball can maintain a low trajectory and a skidding action with the court surface. The basic backhand has little spin, and the pattern is low to high. This gives direction to the ball. The follow through on the slice stays much lower than the basic stroke, and the leg position is slightly higher on the slice throughout the stroke than the basic backhand.

Backhand Groundstroke Preparation Flat versus Slice

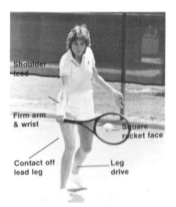 

Backhand Groundstroke Contact Flat versus Slice

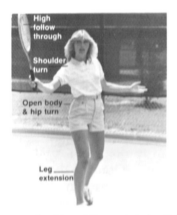 

Backhand Groundstroke Follow Through Flat versus Slice

Learning Experience Suggestions (Backhand Slice Groundstroke)

1. Hit down through the ball slightly under the center.
2. Follow through slightly high with an open racket face.
3. Keep the wrist firm throughout the stroke.
4. Hit high-bouncing balls for a slice groundstroke return.

THE ELIMINATION OF ERRORS

THE ERROR	WHAT CAUSES THE ERROR	CORRECTION OF THE ERROR
Balls that float "long" or hit the net.	Hitting a low-bouncing ball.	Hit the ball off a high bounce or on the rise.
Too much backspin.	Too much high-to-low chopping motion.	Hit high to low, and follow through slightly high.
Balls that hit over the back fence.	Follow through is in the same plane as the contact point.	Follow through across the body with racket face up.

GROUNDSTROKE — TWO-HAND BACKHAND

The two-hand backhand is immensely popular today with people who need the added strength for force and velocity. The player using the two-hand backhand will gain confidence in the backhand and at the same time sacrifice the reach related to a more conventional stroke. With the exception of the lack of reach, the two-hand backhand provides the opportunity to hit both topspin and slice without changing grips; rather, the change occurs in swing action and in the position of the arms in reference to the body.

In the *two-hand backhand,* the racket-side hand grips the racket with an eastern backhand or continental grip at the butt end of the racket. The non-racket support hand rests on top of the racket-side hand in an eastern forehand grip. The heel of the support hand is nestled snugly between the thumb and index finger of the racket-side hand.

Preparation for hitting the ball involves the basic rotation of the shoulders, except that the rotation will be limited due to the two-hand position. The racket is brought straight back and then dropped low toward the feet. The same foot pivot and weight transfer occur with the two-hand backhand as with other conventional strokes, and the subsequent swing pattern is low to high. *Contact with the ball* involves continuation of the low to high pattern with the arms close to the body and the wrists firm. The weight, as with all strokes, is transferred forward to the lead foot as the player steps into the ball to make contact off that lead foot. The *follow through* is a simple continuation of the stroke, with the racket finishing high on the racket side of the body.

Two-Hand Backhand Groundstroke Sequence

There are several significant *differences between the basic backhand and the two-hand backhand.* The arms are closer to the body, the reach is limited, and there is a greater compactness in the swing for the two-hand backhand. There is an extension of the basic backhand when a slice or topspin is executed that includes a swing pattern change. The two-hand backhand has a similar extension, with the topspin backhand exaggerated to a very low-to-high swing pattern, and the slice of high to low to slightly high pattern action.

Two-Hand Backhand Groundstroke Preparation Flat versus Slice versus Topspin

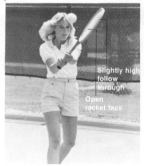

Two-Hand Backhand Groundstroke Follow Through Flat versus Slice versus Topspin

Learning Experience Suggestions (Two-Hand Backhand Groundstroke)

1. Keep the arms close to the body throughout the stroke.
2. Make sure that the two hands are snug to each other on the grip.
3. Study the differences between hitting a slice and topspin two-hand groundstroke.

THE ELIMINATION OF ERRORS

THE ERROR	WHAT CAUSES THE ERROR	CORRECTION OF THE ERROR
Stroking the ball into the net.	Hitting too far in front of the lead leg or not following the low-to-high pattern.	Hit off the lead leg at contact, or at least follow through high.
Not applying any top-spin to the ball.	Not dropping the racket to the feet and bending the knees low with a high follow through and leg extension.	Swing very low to high, and use a low leg bend followed by an extension of the legs.
Hitting the ball off the end of the racket or not getting to the ball in time.	Poor reaction time and little anticipation of where the ball will be hit.	Concentrate on the ball when it is in on the far side of the net. Look for clues that will give insight as to where the ball will be hit.

SYNOPSIS OF THE USE OF THE GROUNDSTROKE

Groundstrokes are the basis to all play in tennis. The developing player needs to grow with the game and progress from a stationary position of hitting groundstrokes to a moving situation that will allow setting up to hit a ball. The player needs to work on both sides of the body equally so that the forehand and backhand can be developed to balance out the skill aspect of hitting groundstrokes. The developing player needs to be skilled at simple tasks ranging from dropping a ball and hitting a groundstroke to knowing where home base is, and moving from home base to retrieve and stroke the ball.

Learning how to *drop and hit the ball* to begin a rally is necessary if a player is going to practice, warmup, or actually play the game. In a forehand ground-stroke, the drop should be toward the sideline and toward the net so that the player has to extend the arm to reach the ball and step, transferring weight to the lead leg to hit the ball. Dropping the ball anywhere else would confuse the player, eliminate the same form development for each stroke, and provide a difficult set up to begin a rally. One of the reasons for a forehand developing more quickly is that the player practices more on the forehand side. This is because it is easier to drop the ball on that side to begin a rally. The drop for the backhand should be attempted as often as the forehand drop to encourage backhand stroke development. The backhand differs from the forehand drop only in that the drop is completed from underneath the racket on the backhand side, and the racket is not already in a backswing position. The ball is dropped in a palm-up position, and a lifting action allows the ball to bounce and come straight back up off the rebound to mid-thigh level to be hit. During the drop and swing, the body is turned to the side, facing the appropriate sideline.

Dropping and Hitting the Ball from the Forehand and Backhand Sides

All practice with groundstrokes usually begins from a stationary position. Hitting groundstrokes from the area behind the baseline is known as *home base*. It is a great learning experience for the player just beginning to develop the mechanics of a sound groundstroke to have all balls hit deep to that position. The rationale for having balls thrown to students in the early stages of skill development or having a ball machine toss balls directly to a player is to insure that home base is identified and that practice be as consistent as possible. There comes a time, however, when the player has to leave home base and move after a ball hit a distance away. The player must leave the home base area, move toward the ball, and hit a groundstroke — then return to home base.

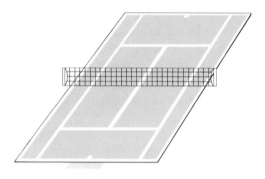

Home Base

Moving to the ball, which involves using the proper footwork, is a major problem for the beginning tennis player. If the ball is hit deep with a high and deep bounce, the player must retreat behind the baseline to get to the ball, set up, then step back into the ball with good weight transfer. In order to respond to a deeply hit ball, the player must first turn the shoulder (remember — the player always starts from a ready position) and take a sideward step with the foot that is on the same side as the turning shoulder. From that point, the movement is either a sideward response or a total turn and run to at least a step

Footwork and Moving to the Ball
Hit Beyond the Baseline

behind and away from the ball. The turning movement must occur as soon as possible, preferably before the ball crosses the net.

Moving to the ball when it is in front of the player is a little easier, but it requires the same anticipation of where the ball is going at as early a time as possible. The player moves in a direct line forward with a timing that will provide opportunity to set up behind the ball and away from the line of the ball's flight. The last part of the movement involves slowing down and gathering the body in a controlled manner, then stepping in a direct line to the ball with the racket side foot first, thus aligning the body to the path of the ball and establishing the next sequential step. That next step involves stepping into the ball with the non-racket-side leg in a timed movement to synchronize with the contact part of the full stroke. As the racket-side leg steps first, the racket is in a backswing position, then it comes through into the ball at contact. There is no difference between hitting a forehand or a backhand groundstroke. The point is to set up behind and to the side of the ball as described when dropping the ball to start a rally.

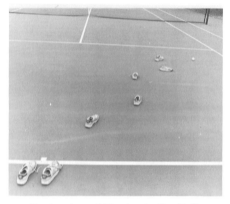

Footwork and Moving to the Ball Hit in Front of the Baseline

If a *foundation* is built from the baseline that is consistent for all groundstrokes, moving to the ball or hitting from the baseline will be enjoyable. The foundation of hitting with a stepping movement, having good weight transfer, and developing a sound stroke pattern is basic. The foundation must be repeated so often that each stroke is an instinctive reaction not requiring thought.

Moving to hit a ball situated between the baseline and the net is not only related to foot movement, but also to decision making. It is now important to recognize which shots require the player to step into the ball, stroke the ball, then return to home base, or to move up to the ball and hit it followed by an advancement to the net. Shots that are hit at the service court line require the decision to continue the advance to the net to play a potential volley or to retreat back to home base. Balls that are hit between the service court line and the net require no decision — the player is forced to move forward to play at the net. When a decision must be made to either attack the net or retreat to the baseline, or when the player

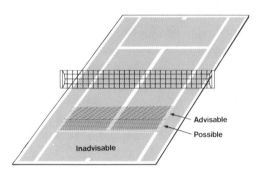

Foundation — When to go to the Net, When to Stay at Home Base

must go to the net, a modification of the groundstroke, called an *approach shot*, has been enacted.

When it is determined that the player is going to hit an approach shot, there are certain perceptions that the player must develop. First, the player must realize that the approach shot is simply a groundstroke that must be moved toward in order for the ball to be hit. Second, the approach must be viewed as a gift given as a reward for excellent play on the baseline that forced the opponent to hit the ball short rather than deep. Third, the player must recognize that approach shots often give the player too much time to decide what to do with the ball, resulting in a shabby attempt at hitting an approach shot. Fourth, the approach shot must be considered a modified version of the full groundstroke swing.

The third and fourth concepts need to be discussed in more detail. Being given too much time to hit a shot allows the player to decide how and where to hit the ball. The problem is when the player changes the decision once it has been made. The player must make one decision on how to hit the ball (i.e. basic, topspin, slice), and another on where to hit the ball (i.e., deep or at an angle). Both judgments are difficult for beginning players, and as a result, they simply bang away at the ball, usually missing everything but the back fence. The developing player is aware of the choices and continues to learn from mistakes, gaining confidence from each opportunity to hit an approach shot.

Modifying the approach shot to cope with the close target area is the skill adaptation to the groundstroke. There are three adaptations to the approach shot from the groundstroke: 1) shorten the backswing, 2) visualize the target, and 3) select the appropriate shot sequence. An approach shot doesn't need extensive force behind it as does a shot from the baseline. Instead of bringing the racket back perpendicular to the back fence, it can be brought back perhaps two-thirds of that distance. If the player will develop a mental imagery of the target as being located at the opponent's service court line, the ensuing distance traveled by the ball will probably be increased by a third of the distance. As a result, the ball will really travel to the opponent's baseline. The baseline is the distance desired for a deep hit, but the mental imagery has to give a short target distance to allow for the short distance that the ball must actually travel. Selecting the appropriate shot is based on the position of the ball to be hit. If the return is hit with a high bounce, the ball can be hit aggressively with a slice stroke to a corner or to the deep baseline (remember to visualize the service court line). Balls that are returned low are usually hit to the backhand of the opponent, with the player then moving to the net to hit a volley off the opponent's assumed weaker backhand return. Returns that hit to the center of the court have a target area of the corners, and returns hit down the line should utilize a slice action as a number one choice. Hitting a ball positioned down the line cross-court opens up too much court for a successful return by the opposing player.

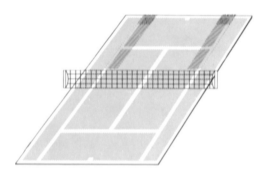

Approach Shots Down the Line and in the Corners

The sequence of moving from the baseline to hitting an approach shot is continued by the player moving on to the net to play a potential volley return of the opponent's reaction to the approach shot. The description of the volley sequence is found in the following chapter.

A final consideration related to the groundstroke is the decision of *when to advance to the next level of groundstroke skill.* When the developing player has established a foundation for success when hitting the basic groundstroke, it is time to advance to topspin groundstrokes. The topspin is a simple extension of the basic stroke, and it can be hit with early success. Some instructors teach the topspin groundstroke and ignore the basic stroke altogether, since the topspin is an offensive shot that enjoys a high degree of success. The transition to slice groundstrokes occurs later, since the slice is more difficult to execute, and because poor stroke habits are quite possible unless the basic groundstroke is developed in depth. The slice groundstrokes are "nice" shots to use, but in reality they aren't required for successful, consistent play. Hitting a two-hand groundstroke is an individualized choice made by player and instructor. Conventional strokes are quite acceptable, and unless there is a significant reason for a two-hand stroke, it is better to stay with the more orthodox groundstrokes.

Chapter Three

The Volley

The volley is one of two strokes hit when the ball is in mid-air prior to striking the court on the bounce. It is an uncomplicated punching action stroke that is also called "blocking the ball." The volley is used in singles play following an approach shot or in a serve and volley combination. In doubles, the volley also is used following an approach shot and as a serve and volley combination, and it is used with a player positioned at the net during a serve. All players must learn the skills involved in the volley early in their development. A singles player may avoid most situations involving the volley, but in doubles play there is no choice but to be located at the net on nearly every shot played.

The volley shot begins from the *ready position* for the ground-stroke except that the racket is held higher at chin level. From this position, the player may respond to either a forehand or backhand volley when located at the net. Part of the ready position is to assume a grip that is both comfortable and functional. The *continental grip* is usually recommended for the volley, since no adjustment must be made for a forehand or a backhand volley. Often there is not enough time to change grips when at the net due to the high velocity of a ball and the short distance from the opposing player. The strength of the continental grip is that the backhand is firm and solid when punching a volley. The weakness is that the forehand provides a weaker base, forcing the player to adjust at the net by changing to an eastern forehand when time permits. Most successful players, in fact, do "cheat" and move the hand on the grip for most volley shots providing that they have the time to not only change, but to also change back following the stroke.

The *forehand volley* begins with a "short" backswing caused by a shoulder

Volley Ready Position

turn. The racket head is located above the hand as the racket is taken back only even with the racket shoulder. The *preparation* is completed with the weight centered on the racket-side foot. The racket comes forward at *contact* with the ball, with the face of the racket striking the back of the ball squarely at the front of the lead leg. A slight downward path of the stroke imparts some underspin to the ball. At contact, the racket head is above the hand, the wrist is very firm, and the grip is tight to prevent the racket from turning in the hand at impact. A step is also taken with the opposing leg, and the weight is transferred to that leg. The knees are bent from backswing to contact. It should be repeated that the racket must be in front of the lead leg at contact. *The follow through* is the final part of the punching action as a short downward motion completes the stroke. The lead leg is still bent during follow through, with the weight centered over that leg. Upon completion of follow through, the player must come up to a ready position in preparation for the next volley.

Volley Sequence Forehand

The *backhand volley* is executed like the forehand volley, but it is easier to mechaniclly complete since the shoulder turn is already to the backhand side and the elbow and shoulder work as a firm backboard when striking the ball. In preparation, the racket head is brought back to the non-racket side and is positioned above the hand. The weight of the body is centered over the non-racket-side foot, and the backswing is short with a firm wrist. At *contact*, the weight is shifted forward to the racket leg as that leg steps into the ball. The racket face strings make full square contact with the back of the ball with a punching action that includes a firm wrist and arm and a tight grip on the racket. Contact is made slightly in front of the lead leg, with the racket above the hand. The knees are bent from preparation through contact and into the follow through. The *follow through* is a continuation of the punch action, with the bottom edge of the racket leading. A small degree of spin is applied to the ball. At the end of the follow through, the weight is centered on the leading leg, and the racket is extended a short distance forward. The recovery must be quick as the player returns to the ready position at the net.

Volley Sequence Backhand

Learning Experience Suggestions (Volley)

1. Punch the ball — do not swing at it.
2. Backswing and follow through are short.
3. Keep the racket above the hand throughout the stroke.
4. Step into the ball if there is time.
5. Stay low on the ball.
6. Hit behind the ball, then follow through with the bottom edge of the racket leading.
7. Make contact in front of the lead leg.
8. Begin with the continental grip, but "cheat" when there is time.
9. Maintain control of the racket with a firm grip.
10. Keep a firm wrist and grip throughout the stroke.

THE ELIMINATION OF ERRORS

THE ERROR	WHAT CAUSES THE ERROR	CORRECTION OF THE ERROR
Balls that have no pace or just drop off the racket strings.	Not hitting in front of the lead leg.	Hit slightly in front of the lead leg.
Racket turns in the hand, causing lack of control of the ball.	Lack of a firm grip.	Tighten the grip or increase the size of the grip for better control.
The ball strikes the net following contact.	Player did not get "down" on the ball and bend the knees.	Bend the knees all the way through the shot.
Ball pushes the racket back at contact.	Elbow and arm are not providing a firm backboard.	Align the wrist, arm, and shoulder in a firm position.

Anticipation is a key to playing well at the net. If the player at the net is afraid of the ball, there will be no anticipation. If the player "sees" the ball early, reacting as the ball comes off the opposing player's racket rather than waiting until the ball arrives at the net, the volleying player will be effective at the net. Once the reaction has been improved, the next important phase is to attack by stepping into the ball rather than waiting for the ball to arrive at the net. Even guessing, as part of anticipation, is better than standing at the net and waiting.

Footwork for the volley is an important aspect of the stroke so that form can be added to the total manuever. Footwork enables the player to step into the ball with body weight behind the punch, and to move efficiently to get to the ball. The first part of the footwork involves a shoulder turn and hip pivot. From a ready position, the player should pivot the hips toward the anticipated position of the ball. With the hip turn, the shoulders will also turn, and the racket side foot will react by pivoting until the body weight centers over that foot.

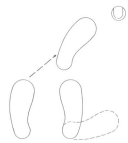

Footwork for the Set Up Volley

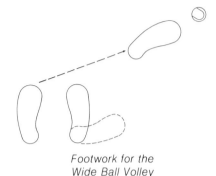
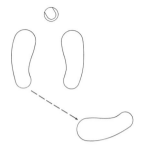

Footwork for the
Wide Ball Volley

Footwork for the Ball
Hit at the Net Player

There are three basic ball positions presented to the volleyer: 1) the set up with the shoulder and hip turn, involving a small cross-step, 2) the wide ball that forces the player to take a lengthened cross-step, and 3) the ball hit at the player that requires a defensive reaction. The *set up* is initiated with the shoulder and hip turn, followed by the turn of the inside of the foot and a step forward and a little across the body with the opposite leg. The *wide ball* is reached by the same movement used for the set up, but the step across the body with the opposite leg requires an elongated, direct movement.

Backhand Volley Set Up

Forehand Volley Set Up

Backhand Volley
Cross Step

Forehand Volley
Cross Step

Volley at
the Body

The *ball hit at the player* requires that the player hit with a backhand volley, if at all possible. The player must pivot off the racket foot and step with the non-racket foot behind the opposite foot to turn the shoulder sideways to the ball. The player must then lean back into the path of the ball.

Body elevation is also important to successful completion of the volley, since balls are not going to be returned at shoulder level in all situations. The legs must be either bent or extended for many of the volley stroke situations.

A *low volley* forces the player to bend the knees and get low to the ball. The hip and shoulder turn must occur to position the shoulder to the ball, and the legs must bend as low as possible. The volleyer steps into the ball with the opposite foot and punches under and through the ball, using underspin to lift the ball over the net. The underspin is achieved by opening the racket face. The closer the ball is to the court at contact, the more open the racket face should be. The follow through of the low shot continues with an upward, short movement of the racket, with the knees remaining bent. Throughout the stroke, the racket should stay above the hand to insure proper technique and stroking action.

The *high volley* forces the volleyer to extend the body and the

Low Backhand Volley

Low Forehand Volley

High Backhand Volley

High Forehand Volley

legs to reach the ball. The shoulder turn must occur early to permit the racket to be taken back a little further and higher than for the basic volley. The player then steps into the ball with the opposite leg and punches down and through the ball. The follow through moves in the direction of the ball just hit and ends at waist level. The punching pattern is a high-to-low closing stroke. The wrist is locked and the stroke is firm.

The volley needs to be *incorporated into the total game* of the developing player. At this point, the volley is an extension of the player hitting a groundstroke and advancing to the net, or hitting an approach shot and moving to the net, or starting at the net in a doubles play situation. The volley is a reward for forcing the opponent into a mistake, and it is executed best between the service court line and the net. The early developing player will play most volleys off the net at a range of one to one and one-half racket lengths away from the net. The more advanced developing player has an increased range back to the service court line, but that same player has the goal of moving closer to the net to be less vulnerable to a well-placed low shot at the feet.

Chapter Four

The Service And Service Return

The service and service return are critical to success in tennis. A groundstroke skill enables the developing player to rally from the baseline. Given the skills of approach shots and the volley, the player can attack the opposing player. Without the skills of service and service return, the developing player is not able to place the ball into play for an actual game, set, or match, or be able to return a service. The three services that are widely used in tennis are: 1) the basic flat service, 2) the slice service, and 3) the topspin service.

THE BASIC FLAT SERVICE

The *basic flat service* is a model for the other two services — the slice and topspin. A *service stance* is used in all serves. The feet are approximately shoulder width apart, with the lead foot positioned approximately the length of a tennis ball from the baseline and the center mark of the baseline. The shoulder is pointed toward the service court target, the knees are slightly flexed, and the body from the waist up is upright.

The *grip* for the *flat service* (and for the two other services) is the continental, with some possible slight variations. The continental grip provides a flat surface for a square contact point. When learning to serve, you may begin by using an eastern forehand or western forehand grip, but you should change to a continental grip as soon as possible.

A skill is involved in *holding the ball for the toss* on the serve and also *in tossing the*

Service Stance

Service Toss Position

ball. To begin any service, you must have two tennis balls in hand. Keep one ball in the pocket of your tennis shorts so that only one ball needs to be coped with during any one serve. The ball to be tossed should be grasped with the fingertips and the thumb, with the heel of the hand pointing in the direction of the toss. From the support base, the ball is placed into a position off the lead shoulder between the player and the sideline, and higher than the reach of the racket. The straight arm lifts the ball from the knee to above the head. The heel of the hand is raised during the full arm movement. As the tossing arm begins the upward movement, the racket arm brings the racket back in a synchronization with the toss. At the extension of the arm reach, the ball is released, culminating the lifting action. The toss must be executed the same way over and over again so that you become consistent.

Service Toss

When first learning the service, keep the feet shoulder width apart throughout the serve. Initially, stability is more important than extra rhythm. Although the feet will not come together in the early stages of learning, the back foot will come forward as the weight transfers toward the target on the follow through.

The first timing aspect of the service is the *toss synchronization as the preparation for the service.* As the tossing hand begins the upward lift of the ball, the racket begins a backward movement with the arm straight. The two arms move in opposition. The racket continues back, with the elbow bending as the racket approaches the shoulder blade area. The back of the elbow is at a right angle, and the arm is in an overhand throwing position. As the ball reaches the

Service Footwork Sequence

top of the placement and begins to fall, the tossing hand will drop away, and the hitting elbow will stay in a right-angle position.

Service Toss and Backswing Position

The beginning of *contact from the half-service position* now occurs. The legs straighten from a bent position in preparation to bringing the racket through in a striking position, with the wrist breaking through the ball. The arm and body are fully stretched. The back top of the ball is hit with the racket face at about four inches down from the height of the toss. The body, led by the shoulder, opens up to the position of the ball at contact.

Service Contact Position

Service Follow Through Position

The follow through continues as momentum carries the racket through the ball and on down to the far non-racket-side leg. A definite weight transfer occurs during follow through, with the momentum of the racket side pulling the body down and forward. This forces the back foot at the last moment to step forward for a balanced finish.

The basic flat service is designed mechanically to hit through and down on the ball. The ball cannot be hit directly down in a straight line unless the server is at least 6'7" tall. The racket makes an upward movement at contact followed by a breaking of the wrist through the ball. Most beginning players have a great desire to hit the flat serve as hard as they can, assuming that the idea is to hit the service with blazing speed. The problem with such a view is that few balls are placed accurately into the appropriate service court, which, in turn, means that the ball hasn't been placed in play to begin a point. The fun of playing the game is decreased and the possibility for success is minimized by first serves that miss the target. The idea is to hit a firm, controlled, rhythmical service that is placed in the service court effectively. Rhythm and ball placement are far more effective than a sometimes accurate, high-velocity serve.

The *execution of a full versus a half-service* requires discussion. Some beginning instruction starts the player with the racket already positioned between the shoulder blades to eliminate the initial take-back portion of the stroke preparation. The purpose is to keep the stroke as simple as possible and not complicate the coordination of the stroke. The choice of a full versus a half-serve is a simple one of efficiency. Some highly skilled players use a half-service position, where many less-skilled players use a full service. Some players are more comfortable initially with a full-service sequence, but all players need to see the half-service position to

1

2

3

*Flat
Service
Sequence*

4

5

understand the upward position of the elbow and the location of the racket during the backswing to permit accurate timing of the stroke.

Learning Experience Suggestions (Basic Flat Serve)

1. Use the continental grip as soon as possible.
2. Time the toss with the take-back of the racket.
3. Keep the tossing arm straight, with the heel of the hand lifting in the direction of the toss.

4. The toss should be higher than the racket can reach.
5. Release the ball at the extension of the arm.
6. Keep the elbow up and at a right angle at the extension of the backswing.
7. Coil the body by arching the back and bending the knees during preparation.
8. Bring the racket through the ball with a slight upward, followed by a downward, wrist break.
9. Let the weight transfer carry the body and racket forward in the direction of the ball, with the back foot coming forward to regain balance.
10. Make sure that the racket follows through to the non-racket-side hip.

THE ELIMINATION OF ERRORS

THE ERROR	WHAT CAUSES THE ERROR	CORRECTION OF THE ERROR
Erratic placement of the serve.	Inconsistent toss.	Toss the ball by laying it off the lead shoulder between the shoulder and the sideline at a height of above the reach of the racket.
Balls served short.	The ball is either hit too far out in front of the player toward the net; the server attempts to hit over the ball; the ball is too low at contact.	Again, the toss must be off the lead shoulder, placed high and between the server and the side-line. Then, the player must remember to hit with the ball at a 4' drop of the height of the ball, and hit through and over the ball.
Ball toss goes behind the head.	Not lifting in a straight line with the tossing arm.	Use the heel of the hand as the lifting agent giving direction to the ball.
Ball served long.	Racket under the ball at contact, pushing the ball up; trying to hit the ball too hard.	Same correction as number two above.
Stepping on the base-line during the serve.	Toss is too far over the baseline toward the net or the player moves the lead leg and foot.	Same correction as number one above, plus the player needs to glue the lead foot to the court.

THE SLICE SERVICE

The slice service involves a side spin, and it is usually used as a second serve in singles and a first and second serve in doubles. The spin permits the server to hit with greater accuracy and still hit a deep placement of serve. The side spin is imparted by contacting the backside of the ball. The result is that the ball lands in the court and kicks away from the position of the server.

The *slice service differs from the flat service* in the toss position and in the movement pattern of the racket. The toss is the same distance

Flat Service Versus Slice Service Toss

Flat Service Versus Slice Service Contact

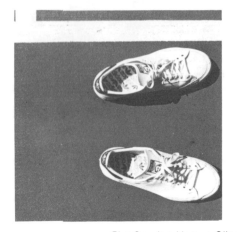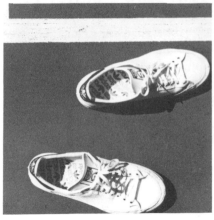

Flat Service Versus Slice Service Foot Position

from the body, but with less height (one of the advantages in the wind is a lower toss for a slice service). The ball is tossed between the lead shoulder and the middle of the body. More spin and less velocity are achieved the closer the toss is to the back of the racket shoulder. The difference between the slice and flat serve toss is that the flat serve toss is above the reach of the racket as compared to the shorter toss for a slice service, and the toss is off the lead shoulder instead of between the lead shoulder and the middle of the body. During a slice service, contact is made on the backside of the ball just below center, with the racket moving from high to low. The wrist snaps at contact with a controlled, firm movement. The shoulders are turned more with a slice service, leaving the body even more open at contact than with the flat service. That openness is due to a small change in foot position, with the back foot placed slightly behind the lead foot.

The *full sequence of the slice service*, including the exceptions identified above, is a rhythmical service with the take away, followed by the contact with the ball, and culminating with a follow through down off the hip of the non-racket side. The weight transfer is an aid to that sequence, as is the leg bend followed by the extension of the leg at contact.

Learning Experience Suggestions (Slice Serve)

1. Toss the ball lower than on the flat service, and toss more to the back shoulder for more spin.

2. Contact the ball on the backside below center.
3. Open the stance more than with the flat service.
4. Use a continental grip.
5. Transfer weight forward through the sequence of the service, allowing the back foot to move forward to regain balance.

Slice Service Sequence

THE ELIMINATION OF ERRORS

THE ERROR	WHAT CAUSES THE ERROR	CORRECTION OF THE ERROR
Lack of spin on the ball.	Toss not far enough back to the racket shoulder; no continental grip; body doesn't open to the ball.	Toss between the two shoulders, or check to make sure the grip is continental, or turn the lead shoulder more through the stroke.
Pulling the ball into the non-racket shoulder adjacent court.	Turning the shoulder into the ball too early, and pulling the shoulder too far through the ball.	Point the shoulder to the service court target area from contact through follow through.
A great amount of spin, but little velocity or distance.	Ball is hit too far back on back shoulder, or racket pattern is too far to the outside of the ball at contact.	Move toss toward the lead shoulder and/or control racket pattern to the backside under center spot on the ball.
Hitting the ball off the racket edge.	Too much of an eastern backhand grip.	Use continental grip.

THE TOPSPIN SERVICE

The topspin is also a spin service, but it involves a downward action as the ball hits the service court target area with a high bounce and depth. The topspin can be used as a first serve, since the speed of the serve can be varied, and as a second serve. The receiver is confronted with a ball that bounces high and deep, forcing a return from a distance behind the baseline or from a high position.

In the topspin, the toss is made higher than the racket can reach, as in the flat service, but the ball is placed directly above the head at least eighteen inches back from the flat service placement. As a result the back will arch more than with the flat serve, and the body will coil with a more pronounced leg bend. At contact, the racket will brush up and through the ball with a low-to-high pattern, striking the ball at a 45-degree angle of racket face to the back side of the ball. There is also an angle position of racket to ball that is based on a clock face. A player hitting with a right-hand position should brush up and through the ball from 8 o'clock to 1 o'clock, while a player hitting from a left-hand position should hit from 4 o'clock to 11 o'clock. This action on the ball differs greatly from the flat service contact position of back-top of the ball. The spin imparted by the action of the racket strings to the ball provides the high bounce to the ball when it hits the service court. The extensive back arch and added coil of the body and legs enable the player to give even more lift to the ball with the uncoiling and straightening of the body and legs at contact. The foot position is altered by placing the back foot in an even more pronounced position behind the lead foot in the preparation phase. The grip

Flat Service Versus Topspin Service Toss

Flat Service Versus Topspin Service Contact

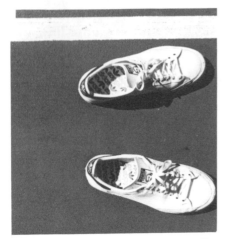

Flat Service Versus Topspin Service Foot Position

remains continental, but a change to an eastern backhand will allow the player to apply additional spin to the ball.

The *full sequence of the topspin serve* includes the variations identified above, along with consistent weight transfer, racket backswing with the elbow up, and racket follow through with the racket finishing low at the far hip. The back foot still comes forward after making contact with the ball to regain balance. The sequence of the topspin service is fluid and coordinated, as all other services, with all parts fitting together.

Topspin Service Sequence

Learning Experience Suggestions (Topspin Serve)

1. Toss the ball above the head slightly higher than racket reach.
2. Bring the racket through the ball brushing up and at an angle on the back side of the ball (the angle depends on which hand the server uses).
3. Stance will be open, with the back foot behind the lead foot.
4. The back arches considerably on the toss, and the body coils with extensive leg bend.
5. Either a continental or eastern backhand grip should be used.
6. The weight must be transferred forward through the sequence of the serve.

THE ELIMINATION OF ERRORS

THE ERROR	WHAT CAUSES THE ERROR	CORRECTION OF THE ERROR
Ball has a flat trajectory or a loft.	Toss was not placed above the head, causing the racket to either hit directly behind or underneath the ball.	The ball must be hit with a brushing up and over action (through).

A *summary of the differences and commonalities* of the three services may be helpful to the developing player. The differences are related to ball toss position, racket pattern movement, and foot position on the baseline and are outlined in Table 4.0. The commonalities involve weight transfer, elbow position on the backswing, wrist

Table 4.0
Differences Between the Three Major Services

TYPE OF SERVICE	BALL TOSS PLACEMENT	FOOT POSITION ON BASELINE	RACKET PATTERN MOVEMENT	CONTACT POSITION ON BALL
Flat	off lead shoulder, above racket reach	even	straight through	back-top
Slice	between lead shoulder and face, lower than racket reach	back foot slightly back	curving line	back-side, under center
Topspin	above head, above racket reach	back foot back	brush up and through	back-top

break at contact, and follow through off the non-racket-side hip. One additional commonality that will enhance the rhythm and timing of the total stroke is a change in foot movement from preparation through contact for the developing player. Instead of maintaining stability with a stationary foot position, the developing player may bring the back foot up even with the lead foot as the racket pattern begins to close on the ball at contact. This small change should be utilized when the player has developed balance and stroke timing from a more stationary position.

THE RETURN OF SERVICE

Because there are different services with different velocities, trajectories, and spins, the developing player may be confronted with a series of decisions related to coping with each type of serve.

Return of serve positioning is a matter of mathematics. The receiver must split the court in half in a line from the server to the receiver. The receiver cannot overplay to the side, attempting to return all serves with a forehand, since a server with an adequate slice serve can place a ball that will kick off the court and out of the reach of the player favoring the side. It is much better for the receiver to position with the potential to hit either a forehand or backhand equally. The depth of the receiver's position depends on the strength of the server and the velocity of the ball. If a player pushes the ball when serving and simply gets the ball in play, the receiver can move up and stand inside the baseline about halfway between the baseline and the service court line. If the server has a strong serve with high velocity, the receiver should stand at or slightly behind the baseline.

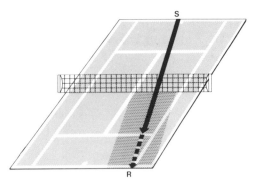

Return of Serve Position

Returning the served ball effectively requires a special set of skills. First, the
receiver should develop a relaxed attitude
and physical position. The ready position,
as a second check, should be high to
permit quick lateral movement and enable the receiver to hit through the ball
with a minimal amount of adjustment.
The third reaction is for the receiver to
rotate the shoulders to a hitting position
at the earliest possible moment. Fourth,
the receiver must transfer weight into
the stroke by stepping into the ball at
contact. A fifth consideration is for the
player to adopt a volley concept to the

Return of Serve
Ready Position

stroke. The backswing and follow through need to be shortened to
a movement longer than a volley but shorter than a groundstroke.
The shortened backswing enables the receiver to control the racket
and bring it through in time to contact the ball. The action of the
racket is a blocking or punching movement that pushes the ball back
across the net, reversing the velocity of the serve. The racket
should be square to the ball and a little out in front of the lead leg,
with a short follow through to add direction to the ball. Sixth, the
racket should be held firmly throughout the stroke, and particularly
at contact. Finally, the receiver must watch the ball as long as
possible up to the point of contact.

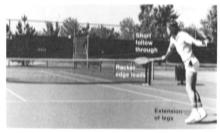

Return of Service Sequence

The receiver must also consider *spin and velocity of the ball*. If the server hits a soft ball (slow), then the receiver, if hitting from the baseline, can take a full groundstroke swing. If the serve is soft and short, the receiver must attack as if the serve were an approach shot. This involves having a short target image and reducing the backswing and follow through. Balls that are hit with a medium to fast pace should be blocked as described under "returning a serve effectively." Serves with a spin present an added complication. A topspin service will bounce high, and the receiver must remember to use a slice return that is high to low. If the serve is stroked as a slice, a block of the ball by the return player will often cause the ball to roll up the racket face or jump off at an odd angle. If the receiver will swing through on the follow through, the sidespin effect of the slice will be controlled.

Target for return of serve is a moot point if the return player is just trying to get the racket on the ball. But with a degree of skill at returning a serve, the receiver can return the ball to spots on the court. The first consideration is where *not* to place the ball. Balls hit short to the server are a reward to that server, so it is important to eliminate short returns. Serves that pull a return player off the court should be returned down the sideline rather than cross-court, and most returns hit soft and "up" should be avoided. This type of serve permits only a certain type of return. If the receiver can remember to return deep with pace velocity on the ball, subsequent play should enable the receiver to gain equal footing in a baseline rally.

Anticipation of the serve is both a physical and mental phase of return of service. The receiver must look at the body language of the server and concentrate on the ball. The body language will provide clues to the spin and velocity of the ball. If the racket face pattern is to the outside of the ball and the toss is short and back toward the racket shoulder, the serve will be a slice. If the toss is off the lead shoulder and toward the net, the ball will be a flat serve. A topspin serve will be interpreted by a toss above the head and/or more back arch than usual. Velocity of the ball can be observed to some extent by the effort made by the server. Concentration on the seams of the ball will permit the receiver to physically react to the direction of the ball. The mental efforts all combine to allow the receiver to make an early shoulder turn and pivot of the feet, thus placing the racket in a backswing position.

Learning Experience Suggestions (Return of Serve)

1. Be relaxed when waiting to return a serve.
2. Concentrate on the server's body language and on the ball throughout the serve.
3. Get the racket back early.
4. Be aggressive and step into the ball at contact.
5. Use a compact swing with a short backswing and follow through except when the serve has slice spin.
6. Maintain a firm grip on the racket at contact.
7. Hit deep on all serves, and hit with a groundstroke swing on soft serves that are deep to the receiver's service court.
8. Soft and short serves should be returned with an approach shot concept.
9. Block all high-velocity serves, and block deep and to the baseline.
10. Return every serve by placing the racket on the ball on every service.

THE ELIMINATION OF ERRORS

THE ERROR	WHAT CAUSES THE ERROR	CORRECTION OF THE ERROR
Hitting the ball out beyond the server's baseline.	Swinging with a full groundstroke swing.	Use a compact swing.
Pulling the ball across the court to the sidelines.	Ahead of the arrival of the ball with the racket.	Judge the velocity of the ball, and time the swing.
Ball doesn't go anywhere after it is hit.	Slice serve.	Block the ball, but add a follow through to the far shoulder.
Ball coming off the racket late with direction toward the near sideline.	Not anticipating early, and as a result, not getting the shoulders turned and the racket back.	Watch the ball, and communicate mental observation to the physical reaction of turning the shoulders and pivoting the feet.
Cannot control direction of the ball.	Wrist isn't firm and grip isn't tight.	Keep a firm wrist and grip at contact.

Chapter Five

The Lob and Overhead Smash Combination

The lob and overhead smash combination are basic for the developing player. Each skill compliments the other in tennis. The lob is an extension of the groundstroke discussed in Chapter 2, and the overhead smash is an elaboration of the service discussed in the preceding chapter. Each is part of the transition package for the beginning learner moving to a more advanced level of play.

THE OVERHEAD SMASH

The basic overhead smash is a flat serve from a half-swing position. The overhead is hit from either the forehand or backhand side, but most players run around the backhand to play a forehand overhead. There are two overhead smashes in tennis — the simplistic orthodox overhead with little foot movement and a simple swing, and the more complex overhead characterized by additional agility and timing. The eastern forehand or continental grip is used for all overheads.

The *orthodox overhead smash* as a forehand is a simple transition from the flat service. The player must maneuver underneath the ball that is hit as a lob, and from that position bring the racket back to the middle of the shoulder blades with the racket elbow at a right angle. The position of the racket physically touching between the shoulder blades provides a reference point for the player hitting the overhead. The reaction that occurs simultaneously with the racket moving to a ready position is for the player to point with the non-racket arm and hand to the ball as a second reference point. The line of the flight of the ball is similar to the ball toss, but the ball falls at a more rapid speed and at a slightly different angle. The bases of the feet are shoulder width apart, and the non-racket shoulder has turned to face the net and the intended target area. In executing the overhead, the body of the player is coiled and gathered, ready to time the stroke. The ball is hit off the lead shoulder, with the legs extending and the body uncoiling. Contact of the racket to ball involves an up and over motion, providing a little topspin for greater net clearance and depth. The racket comes through the ball with a wrist break and a follow through to the far hip, but the action is shortened to accommodate the return to a ready position for the next shot. The full stroke is simplistic, eliminating wasted motion and extraneous actions. The feet remain where they were until the follow through pulls the back foot forward to catch the balance of the player at the completion of the follow through. The player is encouraged to hit out on the ball with smooth, rhythmical timing and control.

Orthodox Overhead Smash

Advancing to more agility with the forehand overhead smash involves adding a few parts to the stroke. First, it is important to set up to hit the overhead. That movement consists of long running strides to get to the general area as fast as possible so that the stroke can be set up with adequate time. Once in the general area, the player will be situated behind the anticipated drop of the ball. At this point, the player takes small steps to adjust to the position of the ball. Balls that are hit over the player's head are handled in the same manner — taking long strides to get behind the ball, then short steps to adjust to the falling pattern of the ball.

The second phase is to use a *scissors kick* for a *jump overhead smash.* The scissors kick requires a degree of coordination and agility. As the player sets up — arching the back, coiling the body, and opening the body with a shoulder pointing toward the target — he/she pushes off the back foot, jumping into the air. While in the air, the feet exchange positions. The back foot comes forward, and the front foot moves backward in a scissors type maneuver. As the legs and feet exchange position, the racket comes forward, contacting the ball slightly in front of the body and off the left shoulder, with the wrist breaking up and through the ball. The follow through is completed as the racket finishes off the far hip, and the feet land in reverse position from their take-off alignment. The scissors kick allows you to gain height so that the stroke is directed downward to gain a greater velocity and subsequent depth and bounce to the ball. The disadvantage is a loss of timing, which may cause you to miss the shot. Many times when a player must retreat to retrieve a well-placed lob, the only shot available is the jump overhead smash; consequently, it is an important skill for the developing player.

Jump Overhead Smash

Bouncing the overhead means permitting the ball to bounce before executing an overhead smash. There are two situations in which the lob is allowed to bounce prior to being hit as an overhead smash. Lobs that have a very high loft are permitted to bounce so that a better timing can occur with the overhead. Lobs that are short at the net, eliminating a good set position for the overhead, are also usually allowed to bounce. Hitting a high lob following a bounce is similar to hitting the overhead from a mid-air position following a lob. The additional time that is generated when permitting a bounce gives the opponent an opportunity to recover, and it gives the player hitting the overhead a chance to place the ball more effectively. The player must set up low and below the short, bounced ball so that the stroke is still downward. The goal for the overhead return of a short ball is a short, hard-hit, high-bouncing ball that carries out beyond the baseline.

The *backhand overhead smash* is used when the player cannot run around the ball to hit a forehand smash. To begin a backhand overhead, the player should use an eastern backhand or continental grip, and turn the shoulder with the back actually facing the net.

Backhand Overhead Smash

The elbow on the racket side is up and points to the ball, while the racket head is below the hand at about hip level. The weight is on the player's back foot and the head is up, eyes fixed on the ball. The ball is contacted above the head slightly in front of the racket shoulder, with the racket face moving through the ball with a strong break of the wrist. The weight is transferred forward through the ball, with the follow through carrying the racket head downward and parallel to the court surface.

The *incorporation of the overhead smash into the total game* blends favorably with the total game plan of a player. The overhead is the second type of shot that is hit before the ball bounces, thus joining the volley shot as a stroke hit near the net. When a player is at the net, the opponent must either hit a groundstroke that hopefully can be volleyed, or a lob that can be returned as an overhead smash. The developing player, with improving skill and confidence, can hit an overhead from any location on the court, while the beginning player should hit overheads when lobs are short between the service court line and the net. The beginning player would also be wise to let the ball bounce before executing an overhead so that timing can aid in the stroke. As skill is developed, overheads should be hit on the fly, and the scissors kick should be added. Regardless of skill development, the player needs to remember that the overhead smash is an offensive shot that must be hit under control and with confidence. The player should also remember that the overhead is a first in a series of overheads if the opponent returns the first overhead. Returns of overheads tend to be shorter lobs than the first lob hit, consequently, setting up the player at the net for an eventually "easy" overhead.

Learning Experience Suggestions (Overhead Smash)

1. The overhead smash is a basic throwing action that imitates the flat serve.
2. The racket head must be placed between the shoulder blades on the backswing.
3. The non-racket arm should point at the ball for a reference point to the ball.
4. The body is turned to the side, and the back is arched.
5. The base of the orthodox overhead is wide and should remain wide throughout the stroke.
6. The racket is brought through the ball with a wrist snap and a downward follow through.
7. The scissors kick for added jumping height and ball velocity is a simple exchange of foot position while the player is in the air.
8. The ball should be bounced when it is lobbed extremely high or is hit short to the net.
9. The racket arm should be pointed at the ball on the backhand overhead, and the back should be turned to the net during the preparation phase.
10. The wrist should be brought through the ball forcefully on the backhand overhead smash.

THE ELIMINATION OF ERRORS

THE ERROR	WHAT CAUSES THE ERROR	CORRECTION OF THE ERROR
Hitting into the net.	Ball is too far out in front of the lead shoulder.	Get directly underneath the ball.
Hitting out beyond the baseline of the opponent.	Hitting too hard with poor timing, or hitting up into the ball.	Get directly underneath the ball and hit through the ball with the elbow up.
Inconsistency in placement of the ball.	Racket not placed between the shoulder blades on the back-swing, and player's position under the ball is random.	Get directly underneath the ball, and always place the racket between the shoulder blades.
Ball is hit off the edge of the racket at the top, or off the bottom edge, causing the ball to hit the court surface immediately.	Swinging too early or too late.	Point the non-racket arm to the ball for a reference point, check the position of the racket on the backswing, and develop a rhythmical cal timing to the stroke.

THE LOB

The lob is an extension of the groundstrokes, incorporating the same grip and basic swinging action. Mechanics do require the racket face to open and lift the ball up rather than hit through the ball. Lobs, which are characterized by a high *flight pattern*, can be both offensive and defensive. The flight patterns are different for each type of lob, and the differences are based on the purpose of the stroke and the amount of spin applied to the ball. The stroke most similar to the groundstroke (and that is actually halfway between the groundstroke and the lob) is called a moonball. The moonball is just a higher lofted groundstroke with topspin that serves as a change-of-pace stroke. The second highest lofted flight pattern is the offensive or topspin lob, which is hit over the outstretched reach of the net player, bouncing near the baseline and kicking on deep toward the fence. The defensive lob, with some topspin, is the third highest flight pattern, and it is a response to a particularly strong return by the opponent that forces the player to lob higher, to "buy" time to recover, and to get in position for the next shot return. The fourth lob, also defensive and with a higher flight pattern, is hit off a strong opposing player return, but the ball has an underspin rotation.

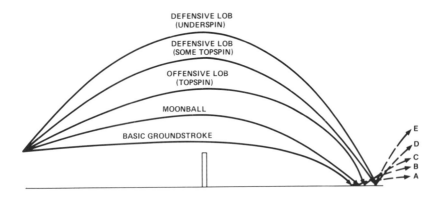

The *moonball* sustains a rally for an extensive period of time and becomes quite frustrating for the opposing player who wants to hit with a lot of pace. The moonball is executed with an eastern forehand or backhand grip and with a tremendous amount of topspin and good net clearance. There should be an extreme exaggeration of the bend of the legs and drop of the racket, and a decrease in the velocity applied to the ball.

The *topspin or offensive lob* is an extension of the moonball and topspin groundstroke. With an eastern forehand or backhand grip, the racket is brought back low with an extensive knee bend. The racket is brought back with the wrist cocked. The racket then moves into the ball with a slightly open face at waist height, meeting the ball from underneath and lifting up. The wrist breaks at contact, imparting topspin to the ball. The follow through continues with the racket finishing at an exaggerated high position off the middle of the body, with a roll of the wrist.

Forehand Topspin Lob

Backhand Topspin Lob

The defensive lob is hit as a recovery phase to an opposing player's strong return, and a modest amount of topspin or an underspin is applied to the ball. The *defensive lob with modest topspin* is

Defensive Lob with Modest Topspin

hit with an eastern forehand or backhand grip, and the the racket travels from low to high. The difference between the offensive topspin and the defensive lob with modest topspin is one of height. The defensive lob is hit high and deep so that the player has time to recover. The topspin is negated with the extra lift of the racket to get the ball high into the air. The mechanics involve a low leg extension that changes to an extended leg extension, longer contact with ball to racket face, and a slight roll of the wrist as the racket moves from contact to a high follow through. The topspin provides direction for the ball rather than a kick out beyond the baseline.

Defensive Lob with Forehand Underspin

The *defensive lob with underspin* is a reaction, in many situations, to an opponent's overhead smash. With an eastern forehand or backhand grip, the racket is brought back into a short backswing position with a firm wrist. The racket is brought forward to hit the ball off the lead shoulder. The bottom edge of the racket leads, opening the racket face. The follow through is high, with the racket face remaining open. The racket stays in the same plane as during the swing from preparation to contact. The wrist remains firm throughout the stroke, and the weight transfer, although important, is minimal compared with other strokes. The legs are bent and extended through the swing pattern, but only with a minimum amount of change. The lob is a reaction to an aggressively hit ball, and the total stroke has to be in moderation to combat the high velocity of the ball.

Defensive Lob with Backhand Underspin

An opposing player may sometimes hit an overhead smash with high velocity that takes the ball deep to the baseline, and the player returning that shot has only one defensive choice. That response is blocking the ball back by hitting a *defensive lob with the racket in an up-block position.* The idea is to establish contact with the ball and block it high back to the opponent's baseline. There is no backswing, but rather a placement of the racket in front of the body with a firm arm and wrist support. The racket face position is angled and flat to the line of the ball, providing a backboard for the ball. A western forehand grip can be used with the forehand block, while an eastern backhand should be used for the backhand side of the stroke.

Defensive Lob with Racket Up In Block Position Forehand

*Defensive Lob
with Racket Up
In Block Position Backhand*

Racket control, weight transfer, and movement of the feet are essential to hitting lobs. Racket control is used to apply topspin of varying degrees, underspin, or a simple block of the ball. Weight transfer, as with all shots, is important with the lob, but the transfer has more to do with the hips and a little step transfer rather than with a long step into the ball. It is more of a center of gravity movement forward. Most lobs are hit on the move rather than from a stationary position. The player is either retreating from the net to hit the ball or is moving laterally along the baseline. As a result of having to hit a lob on the run, the lob isn't always a nice set up from a ready position that permits an easy execution of the stroke. Moving the feet to get to the ball, then recovering enough to place the racket on the ball, while attempting to hold form, are all based on the initial foot movement and anticipation as to the location that the opponent has intended for target.

Retreating to Hit a Lob Behind the Baseline Sequence

The *incorporation of the lob into the total game* is important to the developing player. Without the lob, there is no response to the overhead smash, and the options to hitting a ball when the opponent is at the net are decreased by one. The lob also serves as an occasional change-of-pace stroke, and it can be frustrating for the opponent who likes pace associated with the game or who

Reaching to Hit a Backhand Lob

cannot hit an overhead effectively. The lob is an extension of a groundstroke, and developing the skill is only a transition rather than development of a totally new stroke.

Learning Experience Suggestions (Lobs)

1. Lobs with topspin require a rolling of the wrist from contact through follow through.
2. All lob follow throughs are to finish high.
3. The more defensive a lob, and the more change from some topspin to an underspin, the more firm the wrist and shorter the backswing.
4. Applying an underspin to a ball on the defensive lob requires a follow through in the same plane.
5. Leg bend and extension are part of a lob, but the degree relates to the amount of topspin. The more topspin, the more leg bend and extension.
6. The racket face must be open on lobs at contact.
7. It is important to move to the ball as quickly as possible so that form can be incorporated into the stroke.

THE ELIMINATION OF ERRORS

THE ERROR	WHAT CAUSES THE ERROR	CORRECTION OF THE ERROR
Lobs hit long beyond the opponent's baseline.	Too much velocity applied to the ball.	Control the follow through to the midsection of the body.
Balls hit short just over the net.	Usually not enough follow through and backswing.	If stroking the lob, rather than blocking, the backswing and follow through should be equal in distance, and the more distance, the farther the ball will travel.
Lobs that are blocked rebound off at different angles.	Racket face isn't square to the ball.	Provide a firm arm and wrist base with a flat racket face angled for the rebound. Make sure that the forehand grip is a western grip.

Chapter Six

Other Strokes To Be Aware Of And Recognize

The developing player has been introduced to all strokes that are necessary for a sound tennis playing experience. If the strokes presented in the previous chapters are practiced and nourished, they will serve the player well, and the varietal strokes presented on the following pages will add in only a small way. The important concept is to develop the basic strokes to perfection and execute them when circumstances call for their use.

There are two ball pickup maneuvers that are not really strokes, but they provide a convenient means of picking the ball up without bending over, and there are seven strokes of a varietal nature. The seven strokes are listed in order of learning preference:

1. Half Volleys
2. Chop Shots
3. Drop Volleys and Drop Shots
4. Dink Shots and Dump Shots
5. Angled Overhead Smashes
6. Lob Volleys
7. American Twist Service

Pickup maneuvers are nice to have as part of the player's tennis personality. The pickups provide a picture of a knowledge-able player even when that player's strokes are still developing and there is a lack of consistency. The first *pickup* is a *lifting action,* with the initial stage being a placement of the racket on one side of the ball and the foot on the other side. In one motion the ball is lifted. The pressure of the racket and the foot keeps the ball in control. Once

Foot Pickup Maneuver

the ball is in the air, the foot drops and the racket is used to hit down on the ball, forcing the ball to the court surface, from which it

Ball Bounce
Pickup Maneuver

rebounds back up into the player's hand. The second pickup manuever is a *ball bounce action*, and it is completed by the player moving the racket hand down to the throat of the racket, assuming a western grip. The player then taps the ball with a quick wrist action, lifting the racket up as the ball begins to rebound higher.

Half-volleys are necessary when the player is positioned in the midcourt area and is confronted with a return shot placed just in front of the feet. The player uses an eastern forehand or backhand grip, or a continental grip, and strokes the ball as a combination groundstroke and volley. The player must bend both legs to the extreme, with the lead leg bent at a right angle and the back leg nearly scraping the court surface. The ball must be contacted on the "short" bounce or before it rises. The wrist is firm at contact, and the angle of the racket face is open just enough to permit the ball to clear the net. The backswing is short, as with an approach shot, and the follow through lifts the body up from the low position. Throughout the shot, the head should stay down to insure that the body does not lift early. The forehand half-volley contact point is at the lead leg, and the backhand point is in front of the lead leg.

The *chop shot* is usually executed from the baseline or as a return of service, and it acts as a change of pace response to the

Forehand Half-Volley

Backhand Half-Volley

Forehand Chop Sequence

opponent's placement of a shot. Highly skilled players seldom use the stroke, but at an intermediate level, the chop can be a frustrating shot to return. The continental grip is used for the chop, and the mechanics are the same from either side of the body. The pattern of the stroke is high to low, with the follow through finishing at the feet. The wrist is locked in a slightly cocked position as the racket moves from a high backswing through the ball. At contact, the wrist remains firm, and the ball is hit at waist level off the lead leg. The follow through is completed low and across the body. The only difference between the forehand and backhand is that the ball is hit out in front of the lead hip on the backhand stroke. The ball is

Backhand Chop Sequence

rotated in a heavy underspin that causes the ball to float and hit the court with a biting backspin. The ball must be hit from a high position to have any pace or depth.

Drop volleys and drop shots are touch shots that just clear the net and drop into the opponent's service court area. Highly skilled players disguise the shot as a normal groundstroke to prevent the opponent from moving to the net early and returning the shot. The differences between a drop volley and a drop shot are position on the court and position of the ball. A drop volley is hit from a net position and prior to the ball bouncing on the court. A drop shot is hit following the bounce of the ball, usually from the baseline, and is designed to barely clear the net, landing in a service court. As a rule of thumb, the ball bounces three times in the service court. The three-bounce rule is simply to express the need for touch on the shot. The continental grip is used for both the forehand and backhand, and the racket pattern is similar to that used for a slice groundstroke — high to low to slightly high. The racket face for the forehand strikes underneath and to the back side of the ball, and the ball is hit off the lead leg. In the backhand, the racket contacts the

ball slightly in front of the lead leg and underneath the ball. The wrist for both sides of the body remains firm throughout the stroke, and the head stays "down." The follow-through is initially downward followed by a slight upward movement across

Forehand Drop Volley   *Backhand Drop Valley*

the body to about shoulder height. The racket face is open. The touch of the shot is associated with timing and with a reduction in racket head speed.

Variations of the drop shot concept can be called *dink shots* and *dump shots. Dink shots* are hit with the same form as drop shots with the exception that a side spin, rather than an underspin, is applied to the ball. The side-spin action along the racket face occurs from the top of the racket face to the bottom in a straight line. The forehand arm action brings the racket arm into the body with the elbow just clearing the rib cage, as both wrist and elbow cut across the stomach area. For the backhand movement, the racket head

travels across the
upper torso at an
angle of high to low,
with the elbow lead-
ing and carrying on
toward the sideline.
The *dump shot* is a
placement shot with
no spin. High shots
hit to the net player
are guided to a va-
cant spot on the
court from a station-

Forehand Dink   Backhand Dink

ary position. The action involves a pushing motion with little force
behind the shot and with little spin applied to the ball. The form is
basically a volley pattern, but the ball is gently guided, rather than
punched, as in a volley shot.

An *angled overhead smash* is a combination of the overhead smash
and the slice service. The stroke is intended to apply side spin to the
ball as a variation to high-velocity smashes. The ball is angled cross-
court, and the kick of the ball is away from the player executing the
smash. Once you can effectively hit a slice service and an overhead
smash, you only have to bring the racket head to rest between the
shoulder blades and hit on the outside back of the ball at contact in
order to execute an angled overhead. The elbow should be at a right
angle at the backswing point, and the ball should be permitted to
drop off the face at the same position as a slice service.

The *lob volley* is a combination of the lob and volley shots. As a
special shot, the lob volley is hit when both players are at the net
facing each other. Instead of hitting a volley return, the player
opens the racket face and with a volley action lifts the ball with
topspin over the head of the opposing player at the net, driving that
player back to the baseline. The touch associated with the shot
comes from a nice deep leg bend and lift to give the ball the needed
height to clear the opponent's outstretched racket.

A spin service that is hit on the opposite side of the ball to the
slice service is described as an *American twist serve*. It is an excellent
serve for the right-handed player who wants to hit a service that
responds like a slice service hit by a left-handed player. The ball
moves in a side spin and bounces in the opposite direction of the
slice. The elbow action through the serve is similar to that of a
screwball pitcher in baseball. The twist serve is highly effective, but
it is a potential injury stroke due to the great amount of torque

American Twist Service Sequence

placed on the elbow over a long time. The player needs to be less interested in developing a skill of hitting the ball and more interested in recognizing the effects of the stroke on ball rotation so that it will be easier to return the serve.

For service, the ball is tossed above and slightly behind the head of the server, forcing an extreme arch of the back and coiling of the body. The ball is hit with a brushing up motion through the back side, then with a downward movement of the racket face on the back top of the ball. The racket head follows through off the racket-side hip. The continental grip provides the open face of the racket to allow the brushing of the ball, and the racket-side follow through forces the racket to impart a side spin to the ball. The final action on the return side of the court is a ball that has a side spin and a high bounce kick to the opposite side associated with a slice service.

Chapter Seven

Putting The Strokes Together With Ability

A number of strokes have been presented for the developing player's consideration. You have a choice of grips, including the eastern forehand and backhand, continental, western forehand, and two-hand backhand.Each grip has its own purpose depending on the stroke used. Groundstrokes involve a swinging action and may include the use of topspin, slice, or flat ball rotation. Volley shots are associated with quick reaction movement and a punching action. The service stroke is a throwing action in which slice, topspin, and flat ball rotation may be utilized. Approach shots and return of service are used to handle special situations, and they are a combination of groundstroke and volley actions. The overhead smash is an extension of the service and an attacking stroke. Lobs have been added to the player's repertoire as an elaboration of the groundstroke, and they serve as a defensive and offensive response to an opponent's shot.

The developing player must begin with the basic strokes and progress to the more advanced ones. All of the strokes reviewed above need to be a part of a player's potential skill development, but the progression needs to begin with basic flat strokes and extend to hitting topspin and slice strokes, followed by the combination strokes.

Combined with strokes and grips is the ability to move to the ball. Strokes are combined in a sequence by hitting an approach shot and going to the net and volleying, or serving and going to the net, or reacting to a short lob at the net and returning an overhead smash. Other sequences place a player in a retreat position from the net to the baseline to return a ball as a lob, and from the baseline returning a lob by moving laterally or retreating behind the baseline. It takes time for all grips, strokes, movement, and combination of strokes and movement to fit together in a neat package.

You must be patient and develop each stroke in a systematic manner.

The key to all accepted play in tennis is to begin a stroke from a ready position, and to mentally anticipate where and how the opponent is going to hit the ball. You must understand these concepts in order to *react and get to a ball*. For example, in a groundstroke, your reaction from the ready position would be to begin an early backswing and move a step behind and away from the ball. Once positioned to hit the ball, and with the racket already back with the side facing the net, the key is to step into the ball and transfer weight from the back leg to the front leg. The follow through is the culmination of the stroke that provides direction to the flight of the ball. Regardless of the stroke (groundstroke, volley, overhead smash, or lob), the reaction and movement to the ball are similar.

Stepping into the ball has been emphasized throughout as a major part of a stroke. The idea is to transfer the weight of the body (i.e., the center of gravity) to help give force to the ball at contact, allowing the ball to have a greater velocity as it travels from the racket across the net. Stepping into a ball is a conventional, effective linear movement. There is another less popular movement that also transfers weight forward into the ball. That movement is described as *hitting from an open stance*. With this movement, an angular momentum is generated by body rotation rather than by the linear action of the forward step into the ball. A comparison of the two movements demonstrates that stepping into the ball with the lead foot is completed by pushing off with the back foot, while in the open stance, the player pushes off the lead foot and transfers weight to the back foot as the back foot is planted in a stationary position. The open stance movement is completed when the upper body rotates around and through the ball. The back foot acts as the base into which the player throws the weight at contact.

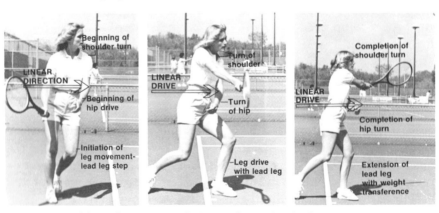

Linear Step Into the Ball on a Groundstroke Sequence

Timing is impor- tant in putting the strokes together, and it requires anticipa- tion and control. The player must per- ceive where the ball will bounce on the court, and where the ball will rebound fol- lowing contact with the court surface. Groundstrokes with little spin are going to rebound at the same angle that the ball strikes the sur- face. Topspin rota- tion of the ball is going to bounce quickly and deeply. Slice groundstrokes, and all other under- spin strokes, will hit the court surface and skid lower than the original angle of con- tact with the court if

*Angular Step and Open Stance
on a Groundstroke Sequence*

hit from a high to low to slightly high pattern of the racket movement through the stroke. Flat overheads and flat serves will rebound off the court with the same angles as the original contact, but it must be remembered that overhead smashes are hit from all parts of the court to all parts of the opposite side of the net, while serves are hit from the baseline to the service court from very consistent distances. High lobs strike the court and bounce up, and topspin lobs hit and bounce up and out with decreased velocity as compared to a topspin groundstroke.

Timing is also related to where the ball will eventually be positioned to be hit rather than where it bounces originally. You must comprehend where the ball will go after it bounces, and set up behind and away from the ball so that you can step into the ball to hit it. Players tend to get too close to the ball or too far away, which causes them to lurch to hit the ball rather than smoothly stepping

*Position of Ball and Feet
Away and Behind the Ball*

into the ball. If the ball is too far away, the player can adjust (and not lose timing), by stepping toward the ball with a weight transfer. If the ball is too close, the player should step away, yet forward, to hit the ball.

Part of timing involves controlling the racket head speed. Players under pressure tend to swing too hard or fast, particularly with the return of service. You must remember to play from a relaxed position and control the racket head speed. The same experience occurs with hitting overhead smashes and hitting groundstrokes when the opposing player is at the net. The added pressure tends to break down timing, forcing the player to rush through the stroke. The focal points have to be relaxation, confidence in hitting the ball, and concentration on the ball. Timing is improved immeasurably by watching the ball as long as possible. This is the part of focus that is most often ignored.

Stepping Into The Ball

Stepping Away From The Ball

Chapter Eight

Physical Aspects of Playing Tennis

The physical aspects of playing tennis begin to play a major role in performance when two players can maintain a rally, keeping the ball in play for a significant amount of time. At that point, you should physically prepare to play the game through a series of stretches and tennis-hitting warm-ups. Prevention and care of tennis injuries are also important aspects of preparing to play the game. Finally, good nutrition enables the player to not only play effectively, but to sustain a physical level during a match.

PHYSICALLY PREPARING TO PLAY TENNIS

There are three phases to physically preparing to play: stretching as a warm-up to hitting the ball, the basic tennis warm-up, and the warm-down through stretching. The first two are designed to actually prepare the player to play, while the third, the warm-down, enables the player to deactivate and decrease muscle stimulation.

When *stretching*, most young players give a cursory effort to preparation of the muscles. However, the young body needs to establish a stretching routine that will be part of the total playing habit into middle age and beyond. It should be incorporated into the player's routine as that player continues to improve and place more stress on the body with extended rallies and overall court play development. The recommended stretching includes some ballistic movement along with static stretching. If the player will devote just five minutes to these warm-up efforts, the risk of injury will be diminished, preparation for the hitting warm-up will be complete, and the body will feel relaxed and prepared to engage in a competitive situation.

Research indicates that prior to stretching the muscles should have engaged in some physical work. The work prescribed is a two-minute run or three minutes of running in place. Following the brief running, stretching should begin with concentration on groin, hamstring, gastrocnemius, Achilles' tendon, and shoulder-arm areas. The groin and hamstring stretch is self-explanatory, as pictured. The gastrocnemius stretch requires that *static* stretch (*not* bouncing) be placed on only one leg at a time, and that the distances

Groin &
Hamstring Stretch

Gastrocnemius
Stretch

Achilles'
Tendon Stretch

for the stretch of each leg vary. To stretch the Achilles' tendon, stand on an elevated area and drop both heels two inches below level for five to fifteen seconds. To do knee lifts, which will stretch the groin and pelvic area, grasp the knee with both hands and lift it as high as the waist. The shoulder and arm are stretched by placing the serving elbow in an up position with the racket between the shoulder blades. The non-racket hand then pulls the elbow of the racket arm backward as the arm attempts to resist that effort.

Knee Lift

Serving Shoulder
and Arm Stretch

The next two stretching activities are really *ballistic* in nature and are familiar to most individuals. One exercise is a series of curls designed to work the abdominal and pelvic area. The legs should be positioned at 90 degrees with arms folded across the chest. The second ballistic stretch, called side bends, involves a simple angular trunk rotation that loosens the hip and back areas.

Curls

Side Bends

The last two exercises are *dry land* ballistic movements that emulate the serving and groundstroke movements in tennis. Both exercises should be conducted with the covered racket in hand. The first dry land effort is a serving motion that follows a non-ending sequence to loosen the arm and shoulder. The second exercise follows a similar pattern but with the groundstroke. The hips, shoulders, and back muscles will be stretched. Both dry land movements should begin with a minimal exertion and increase in speed.

Serve Motion Warm-Up

Groundstroke Motion Warm-Up

The basic tennis warm-up follows the stretching, ballistic, and dry land exercises. The warm-up is designed to increase circulation and respiration, and to provide a grooving of tennis strokes. A good warm-up should last 15 minutes, and at the conclusion, both players should be perspiring profusely. A 15-minute warm-up is often shortened due to a player wanting to start the game immediately or having a limited amount of court time available. The developing player should always work on strokes to be used in the match when warming up. The players should be partners in the warm-up —giving as well as receiving — and attempting to insure that the other partner has had the opportunity for a sound warm-up. The sequence to every tennis warm-up includes:

1. Groundstrokes.
2. One player hits groundstrokes, the other volleys, then switch.
3. One player hit lobs while the other hits overheads, then switch.
4. One player hits service while the other player retrieves the serves, then switch (**note:** there is no return of service — that takes time and detracts from the total warm-up effort).

Although the sequence may differ depending on the location of the players geographically, the concept is reasonably standard.

Finally, at the conclusion of the match and while the players are talking to each other, a *warm-down stretching* activity should be completed. The three stretching exercises identified are:

1. Groin and leg stretch.
2. Hamstring stretch.
3. Achilles stretch.

As part of the warm-down, you should put on a warm-up top and pants and cool down by walking for a period of time prior to sitting down for a rest. As a beginning player this part of warm-down may be a problem, since you have not invested in warm-up clothing, but you should at least put on a jacket following the match. Needless to say, if you happen to have completed a match in 100-degree humid weather, you certainly do not need to put on a jacket.

PREVENTING INJURIES IN TENNIS

There are numerous injuries associated with tennis, and most of them can be prevented. Serious injuries related to other sports —

including concussions, cartilage and ligament damage in the knee, shoulder separations, and neck injuries — are rare in tennis. Injuries that occur in tennis are usually of a mild type that seldom restrict a player's participation, and the few more serious ones often can be prevented.

Certain *common tennis injuries are prevented* with a little attention. *Blisters* often occur on hands and feet and are caused usually by moisture, pressure, or friction. Feet sliding in tennis shoes, a hand gripping a tennis racket too tightly, or hands or feet not kept dry can all cause blisters. Wearing two pair of socks with the cotton pair closest to the skin will prevent foot blisters. Sometimes a player is bruised when hit by a ball or racket. The only way to avoid this injury is to not assume a position on the court that would provide an opportunity to be hit. For example, if the player is on the direct opposite side of the net and the opposing player is about to hit an overhead smash directly at the player, it is prudent to turn and duck. Actually, most bruising occurs when the player hits the shin with the racket on a follow through of a service. A *hematoma* — a severe bruising — is caused by the same incidents. In unusually warm and humid weather, when body fluid and salt are lost more rapidly, a player may experience *cramps*. Cramps involve contraction of a muscle or muscle group, causing muscle spasms in the stomach or gastrocnemius (calf). Prevention is simple if the weather is hot and humid, or when the loss of body fluid is evident. Consume water at every possible break in the action to replace the fluids.

Pulled muscles, including the groin, the hamstring, and the gastrocnemius generally occur as a result of poor stretching, and many can be avoided by going through the full warm-up. A *sprained ankle* does occur in tennis and usually happens when the player tries to make a quick turn without the foot following in the turn. Sometimes a player will jump to hit a ball as with a scissors kick on the overhead smash and land on the side of the foot, or a player will step on a ball during play. Pivoting incorrectly or landing on the side of the foot are a matter of not coordinating effort and physical skill. Stepping on the ball is controllable. Only three balls should be available for play at any one point in a match. If one ball is in the pocket of a player, and one is being engaged in a rally, there is only one ball that either player has to be aware of. But tennis players get lazy and decide to play with two cans of balls — and many of those balls are lying on the court waiting for a foot to step on them.

Knees and wrists are also injured. Knees can suffer ligament and cartilage damage from the same mechanisms that cause ankle sprains. Wrists are either sprained or broken when a player falls over a ball, or a player backpeddles rather than turning a shoulder and running back to a position.

Two injuries that seem to be quite popular in tennis have different causes. The *Achilles' tendon sometimes is injured* by simple maneuvers. An Achilles' can be injured or ruptured by something as simple as jumping and landing on the ball of the foot without lowering the heel or by pushing off the ball of the foot, placing extreme pressure on the tendon. The tendon, if ruptured, sounds like a gunshot retort, and the player becomes immediately immobile. The Achilles' tendon is often chronically sore, since players will ignore the persistent pain and continue to play. Ignoring an inflammation of an Achilles' tendon can cause a more severe injury that can only be prevented if the player chooses to not play. The other common injury is the *tennis elbow* — an injury with status that is also quite painful. There are several types of tennis elbow injuries, with the main characteristic being an inflammation of the elbow. The injury can be prevented in many cases if a player will use conventional form and strokes. Hitting with the elbow leading on the backhand, or hitting numerous slice or American twist serves, will provide ample opportunity for the injury to occur, and prevention involves correcting poor mechanics.

The *treatment of injuries* sustained by tennis players is varied at best. If an injury is perceived as being serious, a physician should be consulted as soon as possible. If a diagnosis indicates rehabilitation of a serious injury, it may be advisable to register with an athletic or sports injury rehabilitation center. Most metropolitan areas have centers that, following diagnosis, rehabilitate injuries. Home treatment ought to be directed to minor injuries. Blisters usually dry up on their own, and the main concern is to make sure that a blister doesn't get infected. Athletic trainers can build a donut-shaped pad that will ease the pain by relieving the pressure point, thus allowing the player to continue the game. Bruises can be handled by the use of cold compresses or ice packs to reduce swelling. Rest seems to be the only treatment for pulled muscles and chronically inflamed Achilles' tendons. An additional help for the Achilles' tendon is to insert a shock-absorbent pad in the heel of the shoe that protects the tendon. The pad is also a preventative and will take some of the stress off the tendon by not permitting the heel to lower as far as is natural. Tennis elbow treatment is restricted to rest or the application of a support. Elbow splints and elbow supports are available to relieve minor pain from tennis elbow, but they will not eliminate the cause. Ankle sprains are treated with alternating cold and hot compresses and require rest to heal. Again, treatment of serious injuries should be left in the hands of professionals.

Physical conditioning for tennis can be as sophisticated as a weight program, aerobic exercise classes, and interval training programs. They also can be sensible for the developing player who is willing to run aerobically, and who will work on agility and quickness drills that have the side benefit of building cardiovascular endurance. If the player will run long distances as part of a tennis program four days per week and will incorporate a sensible exercise program that would include bent-leg situps and pushups, the strength and cardiovascular-respiratory endurance would be adequately achieved. If an individual tennis workout consisting of drills is added, the physical conditioning for tennis would be complete (see Chapter 12, DRILLS FOR THE DEVELOPING PLAYER and the section "tennis by yourself" for the agility and quickness drills that will add to the overall development of conditioning).

Finally, *warming up* should be emphasized as a means of preventing injuries and as a routine to help the body avoid shock when it is going to be engaged in an all-out physical effort.

NUTRITION FOR TENNIS

One of the major reasons for playing tennis is to enjoy the fresh air and fitness that go along with the game. With the objective of fitness comes the goal of good health, and this involves weight control and sound nutrition. To play tennis, you must be in condition and must work at *staying* in condition.

Weight and diet for tennis must be a concern for the player. Maintaining a constant weight is achieved by a balance of energy intake (the food eaten) and energy output (the rate at which calories are burned). A balanced diet includes proteins, carbohydrates, and fats. Foods must contain nutrients that provide energy and help the body to repair itself and regulate its processes. Carbohydrates should compose approximately 55% of a diet with 20-30% fat, and 15-20% protein.

As a general rule, males tend to use more nutrients than females, while females tend to need more iron. Nutrients, of course, supply both needs. Tennis players should be aware of their own nutrient needs and remember to eat balanced meals. They should also remember that weight, although important, is not nearly as important as fat. The average male should have no more than 12-15 percent body fat, while the female should have no more than 27 percent body fat. Every physical education and health department in every college or university can measure for body fat with skinfold calipers, and most of those departments can under-water

Table 8.0
FIVE CATEGORIES OF NUTRIENTS FOR THE TENNIS PLAYER

Proteins	Vitamins and Minerals	Carbohydrates and Fats
Fish	Vegetables	Sugar
Poultry	Fruits	Fatty Meats
Eggs	Bread	Breads
Cheeses	Milk	Cereals
Peanuts		Dairy Products
Lean Meats		

weigh individuals to determine body fat composition. In summary, tennis players should eat a balanced diet of the five nutrients, should maintain weight through a balance of energy intake and energy output, and should be aware that body fat is more important than weight scale comparisons.

Nutrition as related to a match is a major consideration in maintaining good health and fitness. *Nutrition before the match* should consist of consuming carbohydrates and fluids at least two hours before the match. Natural sugars, including apples and oranges, are preferred over candy bars and other refined sugars. Often, matches aren't planned in a systematic manner, leaving the player a brief time to gulp down whatever food is available. Remember that a light meal prior to a match is better than a heavy meal, and it is probably better to play on an empty stomach than on one that is trying to digest steak and other related side dishes. *Nutrition during the match* should consist of high fluid intake to replenish the body fluid loss. Water is the best. Avoid carbonated soft drinks — the sugary carbonation does not meet thirst needs. Drinking alcohol is also not appropriate during a match for numerous reasons — including the fact that fluids should be simple rather than complex. *Nutrition following the match* involves replenishing lost fluids by consuming more water. Two to three hours following the match, a regular balanced meal should be eaten. When you do eat before, during, or after a match, consume energy food with natural sugars. Do not rely on dextrose tablets for so-called "quick energy." Salt also should be consumed in its natural form with regular meals and in foods. This is preferable to taking salt tablets during a match, which will upset the digestive tract during play.

Taking care of yourself should be a slogan for tennis players of all skills and backgrounds. If the tennis player will eat a balanced diet, intake adequate fluids, and use common sense when eating and drinking, tennis performance will profit. "Taking Care of Yourself" also impacts the healing process following injury, and it aids the tennis player in just staying healthy and fit.

Chapter Nine

Etiquette and Rules Interpretation

Part of playing tennis is understanding the written and unwritten rules of the game. Tennis has been played for centuries, and there are certain ways of behaving and interpreting rules.

BEHAVIOR ON A TENNIS COURT

The unwritten rules of tennis are associated with behavior on a tennis court, or, stated in a more proper form, tennis etiquette. The unwritten rules have evolved over the years, and most of them have a purpose as they relate to tennis.

Appropriate clothing for tennis does not require a major expenditure, but proper dress is part of the game. A tennis player must wear tennis shoes rather than a track type shoe or basketball shoe. Wearing proper shoes reduces the chance of injury, and it prevents marring of the tennis court surface (see Chapter 14 for additional comments related to shoes as equipment). Municipal and college courts have rules requiring proper footwear, and players are expected to wear shorts and a shirt to play on those courts. Playing at a tennis club increases clothing expectations to more conventional styles, including tennis shorts or skirt and a tennis shirt or blouse.

Most tennis facilities consist of three or more courts enclosed by a fence, with one or two gates to admit a player. When *walking on a tennis court*, you should wait until play has stopped before proceeding to an assigned court, and you should walk along the fence as quickly as possible. *Talking on a tennis court* is unacceptable except for normal voice tones, and conversation should be limited as much as possible to the match rather than to everyday visiting.

Warm-up is described in Chapter 8 as a part of physically preparing to play. *Being a partner in warm-up* was described as both players receiving an equal opportunity to prepare physically to play.

Etiquette insists that each player be willing to help the other warm-up in a fair-minded manner.

How to return tennis balls to another court, and *how to request a return of tennis balls* are also parts of court etiquette. When a tennis ball rolls across a court from an adjacent court while play is in progress, action should stop, and the ball should be returned. The action should be stopped assuming that the rolling ball interferes with the play, and if it does, then the point should be replayed. The ball should be returned to the adjacent court on a bounce to the requesting player. If a ball is hit on to another court, the requesting player should wait until play ceases on that court, and then with a raised hand request "ball please," followed by "thank you" upon receipt of the ball. Balls hit over the fence must be retrieved, but the retrieval must follow the same court behavior as when entering the court for the first time.

Once the *ball is in play* during a match, there should be no interruptions for hitting practice serves. That practice is part of the warm-up and interferes with the flow of the game if done during the first or second games of the match. The server must always begin with two tennis balls. For convenience, one ball should be placed in the pocket of the tennis shorts and one in the hand for the toss. When receiving, the player should hit only a ball that is legally good. It is poor form to return an "out" serve. When a ball or other interference occurs during a match, a gesture of "play a let" is acceptable. A situation that might make the point is if a server hits the first serve as a fault, then a ball rolls across the court. If the receiver responds by picking up the ball and returning it to the adjacent court, the receiver should immediately respond to the server, "take two." Another form of court behavior is to communicate all calls to the opponents in an informative manner. Verbal forms of communication are "out" and "let." A ball that is "in" is assumed "in" by the continued play on the part of the player returning the shot. A hand pointing up can be used as a sign language for a ball that is out, and a ball hit out of reach of a player that is good is signified by a flat, palm-down motion.

Emotion is to be left off the court! Throwing a racket, hitting an erratic shot after play has stopped, and verbal outbursts should not and do not have to be tolerated. There is an easy way to cope with opponents who behave in such an unacceptable manner, and that is to refuse to play them. Life is too short to accept behavior of a negative type in an environment that is supposed to be designed for fun and fitness. Other unacceptable responses include making excuses for losing while not acknowledging the good play of an opponent, and not keeping score accurately.

Perhaps the most misunderstood part of etiquette is related to a rules interpretation of *when a ball is called "in" or "out" on a line call.* The rule and the etiquette application are simple. A ball that touches on any part of a court boundary line is "in," and any time a ball is wholly out by not touching any part of a boundary line, the call is "out." The problem is when players don't see the ball and start making guesses. There is no excuse for guessing — the call is specific! If a player does not see a ball as "out," the ball must be considered playable, and it is communicated as good by continued play. There never is a guess on a line call in tennis — the ball is always good unless seen out. There is one option available to an "unsighted" player.

If a player does not see the ball, that player can request that the other player make the call. If the opposing player was "unsighted," or doesn't wish to make the call, the call reverses back to the original player, who must then accept the ball as being in bounds.

Ball on the line - "IN"   *Ball near the line - "OUT"*

Besides playing a tennis match and acknowledging etiquette, *viewing a tennis match* requires certain behavior, since a spectator has the obligation to observe a match with respect for the players. There should be no communication between player and spectator, including the often asked question of "What's the score?" The spectator should be quiet and watch the play, and applaud a good point played. Spectator disruptions are not approved for major tennis tournament matches (such as the U.S. Open or other professional tour match).

INTERPRETATION OF RULES OF TENNIS

The USTA *Rules of Tennis and Cases and Decisions,* 1983 begin on page 183. An interpretation of the most widely discussed are presented on the following pages.

COURT DIMENSIONS

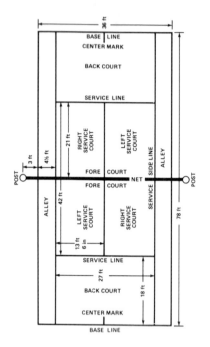

Tennis court dimensions are not important to know except in general terms, but the *terminology* of the court area is important. Key terms include baseline, center mark, back court, fore court, right service court, left service court, service line, and the alley. Important court dimensions are the singles court size of 27′ × 78′ and the expanded doubles court size of 36′ × 78′. The net is 3′6″ high at the net supports and 3′ high at the center. The net height at the center is of particular importance; since a lower or higher height would impact the rally between two players. The measurement of the center net height is done by standing one tennis racket on end and laying the head of a second racket on top of the first racket. The height of the two rackets should equal 3′.

The *choice of serve, side of court, and order of service* are significant choices to make at the beginning of a match. A decision on *choice of service and side of court* to begin play is made by a spin of the racket or a flip of a coin. A racket spin is done by placing the top of the racket head on the court. The opposing player calls either "up" or "down" to signify the position of the butt end of the racket when it falls to the court. The winner of the spin chooses, or requests the opponent to choose, the right to be the server or receiver. The player who doesn't have first choice then selects the end of the court to begin play. The choices may also be reversed, with the winner of the spin choosing, or requesting the opponent to choose, the end to begin play followed by the non-selecting player's choice of service or receiving of serve. A scenario might clarify the choices

Racket Measurement of the Net

available: Player A wins the spin and states, "I will serve." Player B then states, "I will take the north side." A second scenario would consist of Player A winning the spin and stating "your choice." Player B then states, "I will receive," followed by Player A's retort of, "I will take the north side." The point is that the first player has the option of choosing service, receipt of serve, or end of the court, or of passing those choices on to the opponent.

The *order of serve* is a simple alternation of serves in either singles or doubles play. A player must serve through a full game, then exchange service with the opponent at the conclusion of that game. In doubles, the same situation exists except that teams alternate serving following each game. If Team I serves the first game, Team II will serve game two, and the rotation process will continue. Player A of Team I serves the first game, Player A of Team II serves the second game, Player B of Team I serves the third game, and Player B of Team II serves the fourth game. The process repeats itself throughout the set with Player A of Team I serving in game number five.

Changing sides of the court needs to be understood, since it has a significant effect on performance when playing outdoors. Without changing the side of court, one player would always face the sun or wind during play. The opponent would thereby have an advantage. Rotation to different sides of the court occurs when the total number of games played is an odd number. If Player A (or Team I) serves from the north side of a court in game number one, sides will be exchanged for game number two. Player B (or Team II) would then serve from the north side of the court, followed by Player A (or Team I) serving game three from the south end of the court. At the conclusion of game number three, the players (or teams) again change sides of the court, with Player B (or Team II) serving from the south side of the court in game number four. The sequence continues with players (or teams) exchanging sides of the court in the fifth, seventh, ninth, and eleventh total games played. At the conclusion of a set, the players or teams only change sides if the total games are an odd number (i.e., 6-3 for a total of nine games). In singles, the rotation of server is continuous throughout the match regardless of sets played. In doubles, the same principle applies with the rotation of each team in order of service, but within a team there can be an exchange of order of serve at the beginnning of each new set.

In doubles play, there are rules to control the *location of players while serving and receiving*. Once the serving rotation is determined for a team, as described above, the rotation is permanent until a new set begins. The .same is true for a team receiving the serve. One player must always receive from the right service court, and one player must always receive from the left service court. Again, as with serving, change in receiving order may only occur at the start of a new set.

Scoring a game, set, and match accurately is a major responsibility of both players. Scoring when viewed in a systematic order is simple to understand. A tennis match is played in a sequence of points, games, sets, and match. It takes four points to win a game, providing that the margin for victory is by two points. Six games must be won by a player to win a set, with a winning margin of two games. One exception to the rule is that if six games are won by each player, a tie breaker is played to determine the winner, and the final score will always be 7-6 — which is a margin of only one game for the victory. In most situations, the winner of the match is the winner of two of three sets (professional players on the men's tour play three out of five sets in some tournaments).

Each point won by a player is assigned a term as described in Table 9.0. Scores to complete a set are inclusively 6-0, 6-1, 6-2, 6-3, 6-4, 7-5, or 7-6. If a set score reaches 5-5 in terms of games won, two more games must be played. If one player wins both games, the final set is 7-5; if the players split games, the score will be 6-6, and a tie breaker will be played. Examples of a match score are 6-2, 7-5, or 6-3, 1-6, 6-4. The winning player's scores are always identified first in a match; consequently, the 1-6 score of the second set of the second match example indicates that the winner of the match lost the second set by a six-to-one game score.

A *tie breaker* is played only when a set is tied 6-6. There are several forms of tie breakers, including what are called 7, 9, and

Table 9.0
Point Scoring

Point Number	Equivalent Term
First Point Second Point Third Point Fourth Point No Points	15 30 40 Game (must win by two points) Love
Tie Score	Deuce
After a tie at 4 points each — server leads	Advantage In (AD IN)
After a tie at 4 points each — receiver leads	Advantage Out (AD OUT)

12 point tie breakers. The 12 point tie breaker is the most popular, and is presented as follows. The winner of a tie breaker is the first player to win 7 points with a winning margin of 2 points. If the score in a tie breaker reaches 6-6 in number of points scored, then the players must continue the game until one player has a winning margin of two points (i.e., 8-6, 9-7, 10-8, etc.). A 5-5 point score can still produce a winner at seven points if one player wins the next two points. The server for the first point of a tie breaker is designated by the continued rotation of serve per the normal rotation. The first server serves only one point — from the right service court. The second server begins the serve from the left service court. One point is served from the left service court, then one point from the right service court by the same server. In singles, the service order now reverses back to the first server, who begins service for one point from the left service court, then moves to the right service court for the second point. The players exchange ends of court after a total of six points is played, with a continuation of the rotation. In doubles play rotation, movement is the same as in singles except that four players are involved instead of two. Player A of Team I serves point number one to the right service court. Player A of Team II serves two points —one from the left service court followed by one from the right service court. Player B of Team I then serves points one and two from the respective left and right service courts, and the rotation continues to player B of Team II, etc. The tie breaker singles and doubles rotation is found in Table 9.1.

  Placing the ball in play is sometimes misunderstood by players, so a clarification is in order. The start of every game, excluding tie breakers, is initiated with a service to the right service court. The service point, both in a regular game situation or a tie breaker, includes a maximum of two opportunities to hit a legal serve. There is one exception, and that is when a *let* is played. A let is a serve that is hit in all ways legally except that the ball touches the net on its path to the service court. A let permits the server to repeat that one particular serve, and any number of lets may be played in succession.

  Once the *ball is in play*, it must be hit by a player on one side of the court and cross the net on the fly landing in the opponent's court. During a rally, players may hit the ball on the bounce or during flight (return of serve follows the bounce of the ball in the service court). Balls that bounce twice before being returned, a ball hit out of the court boundaries on the fly, balls that hit the net and do not go over the net, and two serves in a row that do not fall into the appropriate service court are all related to a loss of a point. A

Table 9.1
Tie Breaker Server Rotation

SINGLES		
Player Number	Service Court to Serve To	Number of Points
1	Right Service Court	1
2	Left Service Court	1
2	Right Service Court	1
1	Left Service Court	1
1	Right Service Court	1
2	Left Service Court	1
change sides of court		
2	Right Service Court	1
1	Left Service Court	1
1	Right Service Court	1
etc.		

DOUBLES			
Team Number/ Player Number		Service Court to Serve To	Number of Points
1	A	Right Service Court	1
2	A	Left Service Court	1
2	A	Right Service Court	1
1	B	Left Service Court	1
1	B	Right Service Court	1
2	B	Left Service Court	1
change sides of court			
2	B	Right Service Court	1
1	A	Left Service Court	1
1	A	Right Service Court	1
etc.			

serve that does not strike the appropriate service court is described as a *fault*. Servers also fault by swinging and missing a service toss, and by stepping on the baseline during the serve. Touching the service line on a serve is called a *foot fault*. Many players have the habit of touching the baseline in this manner, and legally that is not accepted. If a player strikes the ball, then comes down on the baseline, the serve is legal. When the foot touches the line while the racket is in contact with the ball, or prior to hitting the ball, the serve is lost. In "friendly" play, foot faults are usually not called since they are difficult to see. But the server has a responsibility to avoid the illegal foot position.

There are numerous rule infractions and interpretations in tennis. Some of them are listed below:

1. Hitting a volley prior to the ball crossing the net is a loss of point except when a ball crosses the net and the wind blows the ball back across the net.

2. A ball that strikes the player or the player's clothing is considered a loss of a point.

3. The player may not throw a racket at the ball. The penalty is loss of the point.

4. If the ball strikes the net, excluding the serve, and continues on into the opponent's court, the ball is still in play.

5. If a doubles player hits the partner with the ball, the team loses the point.

6. A receiver of a serve must be ready for service, or the serve must be repeated.

7. An opposing player may not hinder an opponent by distracting the opponent except when partners on a doubles team are allowed to talk to each other when the ball is directed to their side of the court.

8. A player hit by a ball prior to the ball striking the court loses that point even if the ball is going to land out of bounds.

The developing tennis player should remember to treat the rules with dignity and take them seriously so that the game will be enjoyable.

Chapter Ten

Singles Strategy

Strategy in singles is part physical and part mental. The physical provides the mechanics to execute what the mental suggests be done to win a point. The mental is divided into two parts: 1) thinking and broadening thought to plan for the whole match, and 2) using the mind to control the match. This chapter is concerned with the physical or mechanical execution of what the mental suggests and requires in developing a game plan. The mental part related to controlling the match is discussed in Chapter 13.

PERCENTAGE TENNIS

Tennis is a game of mistakes, and the player that makes the most mistakes loses. To win at tennis, it takes a concept described as *percentage tennis*. Percentage tennis is specific to hitting every ball deep and within the lines of the tennis court. This sounds easy, and, in fact, it is if the player is devoted to the system of play. The problem with percentage tennis is that players would rather hit the one spectacular shot than play the ball methodically. A percentage player is one who plays within the limits of skill, hitting only the shots that skill development will permit. In addition, the percentage player hits the appropriate stroke for a given shot. There are two considerations that a percentage tennis player should grasp. The first is to comprehend what shot should be hit from what position on the court, and the second is to understand and be able to apply the division theory of play.

The tennis court is divided into three parts: backcourt, no man's land, and forecourt. The backcourt is a yard deep behind the baseline, and this is where the percentage player returns all deeply hit shots from the opponent. The percentage concept requires that the player be a wall board returning every shot from the backcourt deep to the opponent. The forecourt is between the service court line and the net, and all shots in this area are either volleys, overhead smashes, or approach shots. This is the area that the player should enjoy, because a ball hit in the forecourt represents an opponent's error, which permits the percentage player to control the net area. No man's land is the portion of the court where the percentage player must step to return a shot, then retreat to the baseline to play the next shot. A player should never stand in no man's land. It is a highly vulnerable area and should be avoided.

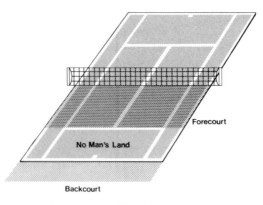

Court Division For Position Play

A second consideration in percentage tennis is to understand and apply the *division theory of play*. This involves dividing the court into two parts on every stroke. If two players are rallying from the baseline and the ball is coming straight back to each player, the court is divided at the center mark on the baseline. If the opposing player hits a ball angled to the left of the percentage player, and the ball lands near the sideline halfway between the service court line and the baseline, and then the return is a comparable cross-court return, the division line for the percentage player, upon return to the baseline, is a step and a half to the left of the center mark of that

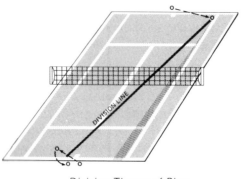

Division Theory of Play

baseline. The theory is to force the opposing player to hit a low percentage shot for a winner, or to return the ball to the percentage player who is situated such that the rest of the court is covered equally with a forehand or backhand shot.

If the percentage player can stay out of no man's land except to return a shot, can apply the division line theory, and can hit each return deeply at least three times in a row, the percentage of the opposing player losing the point is quite high. When hitting from the baseline, the percentage player should use the topspin ground-stroke when possible due to the high safe trajectory and the deep, abrupt drop of the ball at the far baseline.

SERVICE AND SERVICE RETURN STRATEGY

The use of the *service as a part of strategy* is a necessity. Most beginners breathe a sigh of relief when their serve strikes the appropriate service court. Strategy occurs when the serve strikes the service court because the server had confidence, hit the ball with velocity, and had a plan as to where the ball would be placed in the service court. If a server can repeatedly hit a serve with a modest amount of speed and place the ball in the corners of the opponent's service court 70 percent of the time, the chances for success are greatly enhanced. If spin, with accuracy, can be applied to the ball during service, a variety of serves can be used to confuse the receiver. In addition, the server can capitalize on the receivers weaknesses in returning a serve if those weaknesses can be recognized.

Placement of the service should be deep. Then choices can be made as to where the ball should be directed to cause the most problems for the receiver. If the receiver is right-handed and has a weak backhand, the left corner of the right service court and the left corner of the left service court might be advantageous to the server. If the receiver moves to the left to protect against returning a backhand, the server can place the next serve to the right of both service courts out of the reach of the receiver. If a server has a reasonable velocity on a flat serve, the receiver will have problems if the ball is placed directly in front of the body, particularly if the player is tall or slow. A slice serve can be hit wide to the right side of the right service court, pulling the receiver off the court and consequently opening the whole court for the next shot by the server. Serving a topspin serve to the right side of the right service court pulls the receiver to the middle of the court, forcing the receiver to return the ball straight back down the middle of the court. Serving a topspin serve to the left corner of the left service court pulls the receiver off the court for an easy put away by the server. A slice service to the right corner of the left service court pulls the receiver to the middle of the court, causing a down-the-middle return.

The second serve is even more important in the sense that if it is not accurately placed in the appropriate service court, the point is lost without a response from the receiver. The second serve not only must be reliable and accurate, but should have some pace associated with the stroke. Many servers make the mistake of pushing the ball into the service court rather than hitting with good form. The three points required for a sound second serve are: 1) the serve must have accuracy coupled with pace, 2) the serve must have spin to insure accuracy, and 3) the serve must never be pushed or blooped into the service court. Accuracy is enhanced by a slice or topspin service with some attention to placement of the ball and pace.

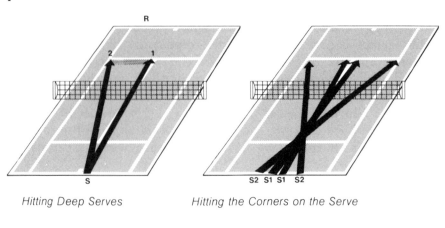

Hitting Deep Serves   Hitting the Corners on the Serve

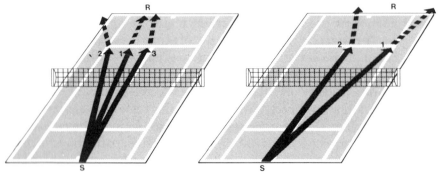

Placing Topspin and Slice Serves to   Placing Topspin and Slice Serves to
the Right Service Court   the Left Service Court

Return of service is a crucial part of strategy. The server's role is to place the ball in play, and the return player's role is to keep the ball in play. The strategy is to hit the ball back with pace, and to hit it deep to eliminate the initial advantage of the server. The server who relies on the serve to win points will begin to lose confidence if the ball keeps coming back.

There is a cause-effect relationship which implies that the receiver should respond to the server's pace and depth of serve by standing beyond the baseline to return serve. Part of understanding strategy is to dispel such thought. If the server has a strong spin, it is best to step inside the baseline and cut down the sidespin or high bounce before the effect can occur. A serve that is pushed over the net should be returned firmly and deeply, and the receiver should avoid the tendency to "kill" the ball. The receiver can use various placements when returning the serve that will enhance the play at that point. Returning down the line is usually a mistake when the server stays on the baseline. A shot down the line will leave the court open for a cross-court winner by the server. Most service returns are most effective when hit back along the flight of line of the serve, and when hit at the feet of the server. When serves are hit with little pace, the receiver has more options, including down the line, cross-court, and angled cross-court. The effort off a weak serve should be to hit a winner under control, forcing the opposing server to hit while moving to the ball, or to miss the ball entirely.

ATTACKING THE NET AND BEATING THE NET PLAYER

Judgments that must be made by a player include when to go to the net, and, once there, when to stay and when to leave. There are three situations in which a player should go to the net: 1) off a serve, 2) off an approach shot, and 3) off a firmly hit groundstroke that forces the opponent to move behind the baseline when returning the shot. When at the net, there are two times to stay and continue play at the net: 1) when following one volley with another, and 2) when hitting an overhead smash from between the service court line and the net. Retreat occurs in only one situation — when a lob is hit deep to the baseline, compelling the net player to leave the net to return the lob. There is one exception to the retreat plan. When the retreating player hits an offensive or topspin lob as a return, that player should attack the net, since the opponent is in a moving position with the back to the net. The player attacking the net should apply the *Division Line Theory* by following the path of the ball to the net, consequently dividing the court in half between the two players. The division line will enable the net player to cover all territory equally between the forehand and backhand and give the opponent only one possible winning shot. If, as an example, the net player hits to the deep, right baseline corner of the opponent and takes a step and a half to the left of the center of the net, the only possible return for a winning shot is to the far right corner angled at the net.

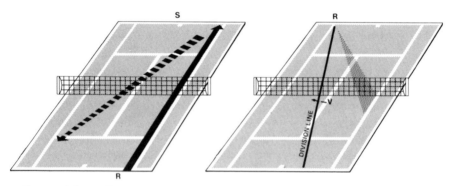

*Return of Serve Down
the Line Consequences*   *Division Line Theory*

Going to the net following a serve suggests the execution of an accurate serve. A serve with pace provides the opportunity to go to the net, since the return of serve may be weak, but the high velocity eliminates deep penetration to the net by the server. If a server can get to the service court line when following a paced serve, then penetration is as close as it is going to be. If the return of serve is a miss hit, the server can pounce on the return with an effective volley twenty feet from the net. If the return of serve is at the feet of the server, who has advanced on the net, a twenty-foot return distance from the net may become a liability. The server now has to be an exceptional volleyer, since the ball at the feet creates vulnerability. A slice service permits the player to advance closer to the net before being forced to stop and respond to the opponent's return of serve. A topspin serve is excellent to attack the net on, because it forces the receiver to hit a high-bouncing ball, thus keeping the ball up above the net on the return. It also allows the server to advance closer to the net than would a paced serve, since the topspin serve is a little slower and bounces much deeper.

Going to the net following an approach shot is an ideal time to advance on to the net. If the return from the opponent is short — at the service line in the middle of the court — the approach shot can be played to the corners. Once the ball is hit to the corner, the player advances to the net, in line with the ball, and volleys cross-court. If a return shot is hit to the service line, close to and parallel to a sideline, the approach shot

Serve and Volley Footwork When Attacking the Net

should be down the sideline followed by a short angled volley cross-court as the player advances on to the net.

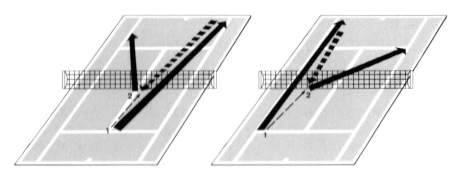

Going to the Net Following an Approach Shot from the Middle of the Court   *Going to the Net Following an Approach Shot from the Sideline Area of the Court*

Going to the net off a groundstroke must be done with some prudence. It is inadvisable to go to the net when the groundstroke 1) has not been hit with authority, 2) has not been hit deep to the baseline, and 3) has not forced the opponent to return the shot while moving away from the net. However, if the player has hit an effective groundstroke, then that player must learn to *close in on the net.* As the player advances to the net from the baseline, a ready position must be assumed prior to the return shot crossing the net. Once a return has been hit by the advancing player, that player continues on to the net in a line with the ball, and again stops in a ready position before the return shot crosses the net. It takes between two and three stops to gain control of the net and be in control of hitting a winning shot if the opponent is able to respond with some degree of authority in returning the shots hit by the advancing player. Three thoughts should be on the mind of the player advancing from the baseline: 1) volley and advance, 2) punch the ball deep to the baseline, and 3) hit at the feet of the opponent so that the return is "up."

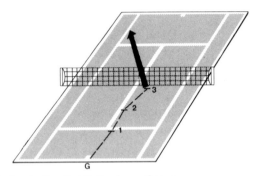

Going to the Net Following a Serve

Advancing to the net is an adventure and a reward if the end result is a winning shot. The choice of going to the net is made based on the advantage that it will give the player to advance. There are some final thoughts associated with attacking the net. First, the volleyer must always stop and assume a ready position prior to the return shot crossing the net. Second, when attacking, the player should follow the path of the ball to provide the division line. A third thought is to get close to the net to hit a volley. A beginning player needs to be a racket and a half length away from the net, while a skilled player can volley from the service court line. All players who volley must remember to stay low and punch the ball.

There is a *threefold strategy to beat the player who attacks the net:* 1) hit at the feet of the net player, 2) hit a passing shot, and 3) hit a lob.

Hitting at the feet of the net player forces the player to hit the ball up in the air, providing a set up to hit a winning return. Two shots are most often used to hit at the feet of a player at the net. A topspin stroke is usually hit from the baseline to the feet of a player at the net, and from a serve, a ball is often blocked back to the feet of an advancing net player.

Hitting a passing shot to beat a net player is a second means of defeating the volleyer at the net. The passing shot may be hit down the line or as a short-angled cross-court shot. As an example, if a player is to the left of the center mark at the baseline, a shot down the net player's right sideline could pass that player. A ball hit further to the left of the baseline player can be played as a short-angled cross-court passing shot, since the net player has moved to the right of center to establish the division line.

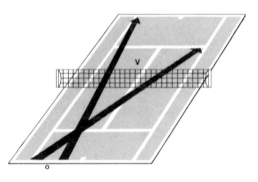

Hitting a Passing Shot to Beat a Net Player

The third method of *beating the net player is with a lob.* A net player tends to get too close to the net to avoid hitting balls at the feet. When this happens, the ability to retreat and cover a deep lob is diminished, and the player at the baseline has a clear-cut choice of hitting an offensive, topspin lob to the opponent's baseline. If the players are beginners, any form of a lob that gets over the head of the net player will be effective. The important point is to drive the opponent back from the net, insuring a return on the move with the back to the net.

LOB AND OVERHEAD SMASH STRATEGY

Hitting lobs as both offensive and defensive shots is an important part of strategy. The question in singles play is *when to hit a lob, and what kind to hit.* Defensive lobs should be hit whenever the opponent has forced the play, and whenever a player needs to buy time to recover from a strong shot. The important part of a defensive lob is to hit to the opponent's backhand, forcing the opponent to run around the ball to hit an overhead smash, or to return the ball going away from the net with a backhand stroke. There is a particular way to chase a lob for a return that helps a player to recover from a lob more readily. When retrieving a lob, the player, instead of running in a straight line, should run to the outside of the ball and come from behind it to either hit a return lob, a forceful groundstroke, or an overhead smash. A topspin lob that has the effect of an offensive shot should, of course, be hit when the opposing net player is too close to the net.

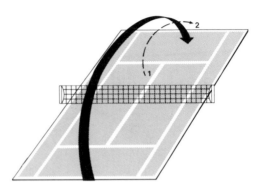

Retrieving a Lob

There are a few *change of pace tactics* that can be incorporated into a lob strategy. One approach is to hit moonballs to an opponent. A soft, topspin ball with a high trajectory often can be frustrating for an opponent who has just become grooved to a certain paced ball. Hitting high, defensive lobs has a similar effect, particularly when the opponent sets up to hit an overhead smash and misses. A few missed overheads create doubt and a seeping lack of self-confidence, which, in turn, creates a frustration and anger that can cause a total collapse of the players game. As skill increases, a player can gain control of an opponent, both physically and mentally, by moving that opponent to various spots on the court. One scenario is to begin with a down-the-line groundstroke followed by a drop shot when the player returns the ball. As the opponent reacts and returns the drop shot, a topspin lob will drive the opponent back to the baseline. The concluding response is to advance to the net and hit the opponent's return of the lob cross-court at a short angle. The play could continue indefinitely if the opponent is in excellent shape and a strong player, but breakdown is both physical and mental regardless of the winner on a given point. If the player can win the point and wear the opponent down physically at the same time then the opponent is mentally controlled as well. Remember — this is just one scenario that uses the lob effectively. Many strategies could be developed incorporating any series of strokes.

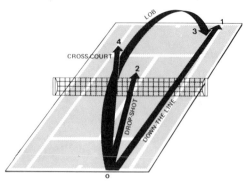

Moving an Opponent

    Overhead smashes are used in singles strategy to respond to lobs that are hit between the service court and the net. Setting up is an important part of that strategy. A crisp volley down the opponent's right sideline forces that player to execute a lob that travels to the middle of the court, which, in turn, can be hit as an overhead smash to the opponent's left corner. This example illustrates that a firm offensive shot creates a weak lob return, and for each lob return, there are a variety of targets for the overhead smash. Balls hit deep to the opponent's baseline are always acceptable as effective overheads. When the return lob is closer to the net, smashes can be angled and bounced out of the opponent's court. The angle and bounce carry the ball into a non-returnable location. Angles and deeply angled overhead smashes are also effective. They insure that the opponent has to move to retrieve the overhead, rather than remain stationary and hit a lob with control. An angled overhead is an excellent placement for a backhand overhead, since it is more important to be accurate in placement rather than fast for successful completion of the shot.

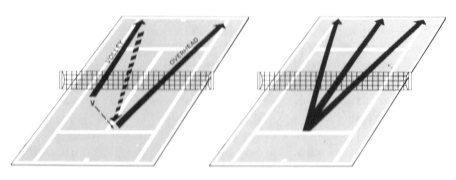

Setting Up an Overhead Return   *Hitting Overheads Deep*
   with a Volley Shot

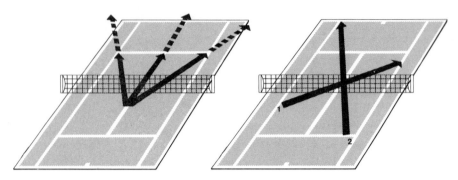

Hitting Angled Overhead Smashes   *Angled and Deeply Angled*
Overhead Smashes

Often the first overhead smash is not a winning shot, nor should it be expected to be. The first overhead "softens" up the opponent, who can only return the shot from a defensive position. Strategywise, if the player hitting the lob keeps the overhead consistently deep and angled, the opponent returning lobs eventually wears down, or breaks down skillwise, and hits a short lob that can be returned as a winning overhead.

BASELINE PLAY STRATEGY

Baseline play involves giving complete, undivided attention to hitting groundstrokes deep, and relying on percentage tennis to its fullest. The idea is to force the opponent to make a mistake with a miss hit shot or poorly hit return. There are several ways of forcing an error from the opponent, including cross-court and down-the-line shots. Duplicating the opponent's return is good strategy because it puts pressure on the opponent to change the direction of the ball. Singles strategy dictates that if the opponent hits cross-court the player should return cross-court until the opponent hits down the line. At that point, the player has the option of returning in duplication down the line or coming back cross-court. In either case, the advantage is with the player as opposed to the opponent, since the return angle favors the player's stroke, and because there is an element of the unknown in the return direction.

Another type of strategy is to move the opponent back and forth across the baseline, forcing alternate forehand and backhand returns. If the opponent can be driven from one side of the court to the other, reaching for shot returns, eventually the ball will be returned short or "up" so that an approach shot, volley, or overhead can be used as a follow-up to good baseline play. With skill and experience, the baseline player can develop strategy using varied strokes, always coming back to hit with depth and angle that will cause the opponent to make a mistake. Sometimes varying the stroke is disguised by hitting down that sideline with a slice groundstroke to the opponent's backhand for a succession of shots, then switching to a topspin cross-court shot that pulls the opponent out of a groove and requires a totally new stroke in the rally. Hitting the groundstroke over and over again to the same side will also wear down an opponent's confidence, and the skill of the stroke will weaken as the belief in winning the point lessens.

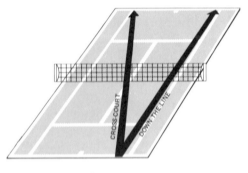

Baseline Play

There are *certain scoring situations* in a match that are vital to good strategy and success. In a game, a score of 30-15 is important. If the next point is won, the score will be 40-15, and there is a two-point difference for the leading player to use to an advantage. If the 30-15 score becomes 30-30, either player may win the next two points. A set score of 5-3 with the opponent serving is a crucial situation in the ninth game. If the opponent wins that game, the set is over at a 6-3 score. If the receiver of serve wins the ninth game, the score becomes 4-5, and the player who is behind serves with a tie set possible at 5-5 in the tenth game. Obviously, the 4-5 set score is also important, but the player behind is serving, and with a degree of serving skill, the server has the advantage. Other scores that are meaningful are the first point of any given game, or the last point of a game, set, or match.

The *overall game strategy and plan* are only as good as the skill of the player. The game plan for an early beginner is to do the best possible to return shots back across the net. By the time the player can hit with some consistency, percentage tennis really becomes important. It means that the developing player can work at hitting the ball back with depth and patience and begin to set up an opponent with subtle techniques to force an error. Continual maturation permits the player to understand that the mind is the most important part of the game. The ability to out-think the opponent becomes the key to victory. Changing pace, moving a player along the baseline, and moving the opponent to the net and back away from the net all begin to make sense.

The game plan and strategy for a player start with the warm-up and end with the last point of the match. In the warm-up, the player begins to assess the opponent's ability, being careful not to become overly confident of or intimidated by the opponent. During the warm-up, each player should determine the skills of the opponent and what strokes that opponent is capable of hitting effectively. It should be cautioned that the player who is assessing should not change the game plan only to meet the opponent's skills. The assessing player must be able to react in a normal manner and not play as the opponent dictates. An example of a game plan is that if the opponent likes to serve and volley, the strategy would be to prepare to hit passing shots, lobs, and groundstrokes at the opponent's feet. Another example would be to stay at home base during a rally and force the opponent to rally from the baseline when the opponent lacks consistency in hitting groundstrokes. Game plans and strategy should be a combination of the player reacting to the opponent's weaknesses, and playing to the level of skills possessed.

Final game strategy thoughts include playing every point and returning every shot. Second, look for the short ball, and attack with an aggressive approach shot, completing the attack by continuing on to the net. Third, be consistent in play rather than hit the one spectacular shot. Fourth, remember that defensive lobs "buy time" and that most tennis players cannot hit solid overheads in reacting to a lob. Finally, if a player will keep all groundstrokes in play and deep, and hit all serves with pace and accuracy, the possibilities for success increases greatly.

Chapter Eleven

Doubles Strategy

Doubles strategy is entirely different from singles strategy with the exception of the strokes that are used. Doubles is an attacking game; singles a more passive defensive game. Doubles play is located at the net or retreating from the net, while singles play is positioned at the baseline. The attacking concept of doubles provides an exciting type of match filled with shots executed quickly and with good reactions. The beginner seldom experiences the challenge of the game, yet this is the first type of situation that a beginner may face if being taught in a college class or in any group, since only a few courts are available with a large group. The developing player can get a sense of playing doubles and begin to develop the attacking skills necessary to success.

BASIC ALIGNMENTS AND FORMATIONS

There are numerous formations related to doubles play, including club or recreational social doubles (usually college class doubles), conventional doubles, mixed doubles, and Australian doubles. Choosing a partner and deciding where each partner will be aligned on the court are part of good strategy in that individual skills can be used to the advantage of a team.

The beginning player should start from one of two formations, depending on how advanced the players are in executing strokes. These formations are associated with *social doubles.* If the players have yet to be introduced to net play, including volleying and overhead smashes, it is best to begin doubles play at the baseline. It is ridiculous to place players at the net who do

Up and Back Doubles Formation

not have the skill to protect themselves or to hit a volley or overhead smash. The second formation is *one up and one back*. This alignment is used when the players net experience is at least adequate for protection at the net, and for execution of firmly hit volleys.

The *two back formation* is used for experienced players when the opposing team is at the net hitting overhead smashes while the two

on the baseline team attempt to return lobs to defend against the overheads. The weakness of the two back formation is the defensive stature of the team and their lack of control at the net. A team that controls the net has an open court that will allow large areas in which to place the ball for winning shots. From the baseline, shots hit at players controlling the net have little potential for success because they involve only small target areas that cannot be covered at the net by

Two Back Doubles Formation   the two players.

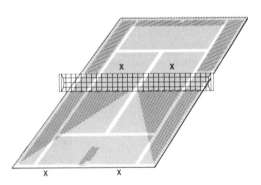

Target Areas for Two Up versus Two Back

One player up and one player back occurs due to the original alignment of the players in the serving positions. The problem occurs when the server doesn't have the confidence to serve and follow the serve to the net, or the return player does not follow the return to the net. Once the alignment holds at one up-one back, that alignment becomes vulnerable to open area winning shots.

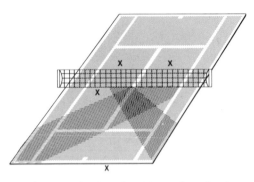

Target Areas for Two Up Against One Up — One Back

Conventional doubles requires that a team attack the net, and, if need be, attack face to face with the opposing team. The key to good doubles play is to work together in a tandem. If the ball is lobbed deep when the team is at the net, they must retreat together, and when one player hits an overhead smash from the service court line, they both must advance to the net together. Playing conventional doubles is working as a team, knowing where the other player is located, and depending on the partner to hit the appropriate shot. When controlling the net, the doubles team attacks side by side, positioning themselves in the middle of the two service courts. From that position, as if they were on a string, they move up and back and side to side in a balanced position.

Conventional Doubles Formation

There are a significant number of movement patterns on the court from a conventional formation. First, a teammate may *poach* in doubles. The definition is important. The poach is hitting a winning volley; there is no margin for error. The net player steps across parallel to the net to hit a volley directed toward the partner at the baseline following a serve. The serving partner sees the poach attempt and veers to replace the position vacated by the poaching partner.

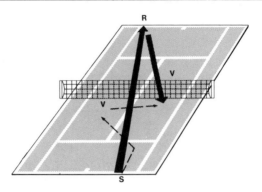

Poach Movement Patterns

Another team movement pattern is to retreat to hit a lob, then recover for the next shot. The retreat incorporates a cross-action by team members to reach the ball. If the lob is to the left deep corner of the baseline, the partner on the right can see the ball and react to it better than the partner who would have to retreat in a straight line with the back to the opponents. At this point, the partners are now at the baseline where they will remain in a defensive posture until they can regain an advantage and return to the net.

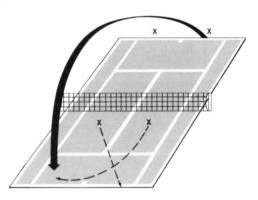

Retreating to Hit a Lob Movement Pattern

Mixed doubles is a combination of one male and one female partner, and the formation used is the same as for conventional doubles. The only real change is related to the physical strength of the female partner. If there is a strength difference (the strength difference could be found with 2 male or 2 female partners), the alignment may have to be adjusted. The reality of mixed doubles is that the female is attacked as often as possible by the opposing team. When a female player serves to a female opponent, the male at the net must poach whenever possible. With the female serving, the velocity or pace of the serve is not usually as great as when the male partner serves; consequently, the female server must stay in an up-back alignment. That alignment has already been identified as a weak formation, and it is the reason for the male partner poaching. A serve to the backhand of the return player will aid the serving team by making it easier to poach by the male partner, and easier for the female partner to respond to a groundstroke return.

When receiving against the female server, several responses can be made. One may be a direct return back to the male net player. If successful, the male partner will eventually retreat to the baseline to avoid being hit by a return of serve. A second strategy is to return serve cross-court. This subjects the server to returning a groundstroke from a defensive position, and avoids the male partner at the net.

Mixed doubles is a delightful game, and it can be highly competitive. Each partner has a role to play and a responsibility to fulfill. Strategy for mixed doubles can be enlarged to cover any doubles where the characteristics are similar. If one partner is a physically stronger partner but the players are of the same sex, the same approach to strategy should be used.

There is also a service formation that can help a team in special situations. *Australian doubles* eliminates an opposing team's cross-court return. The alignment is the server and net player situated in a perpendicular line to the net. If the server is serving to the opposing team's right service court, the server will be to the right of the center mark, and the net partner will be set up on the inside center of the serving team's right service court. This alignment leaves the left service court of the serving team open during the serve. Following the serve, the baseline server moves to the left to cover the open court from the baseline. The partner at the net stays to create an up-back situation.

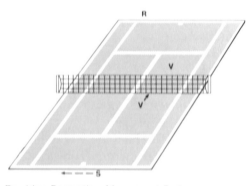

Australian Doubles Formation Movement Pattern

There are several options with the Australian formation. The first is for the net player to cross to the left service court following the serve, while the serving partner moves further to the right side of the baseline to protect that side of the court. A second option is for the team to crisscross following the serve, with the net player moving to the left and the server going straight to the net from the right side. A variation of the crisscross would be for the server to follow the serve to the net on the left side, with the net player staying in the same position.

The more variations the Australian doubles formation can offer to the opposing team, the more confused they can become, and the more chance for success. This formation is ideal for the team with one weak serving partner or a team with one partner who has a major skill weakness that can be hidden by the alignment.

Australian Doubles Formation

WHO PLAYS WHERE AND WHY

It must be determined which partner plays which side of the court on return of serve, who serves first for a team, and how partners will communicate.

There are three possibilities for *who plays which side of the court on return of service.* One thought is that the strongest backhand plays the left side of the court when the team members are both right-handed. With a left-handed and right-handed combination, the left-handed player may play the left side so that the outside of the court is protected on both sides. A third view is to position the strongest player on the right side of the court. The first two thoughts are similar. The strong backhand will lend support to what is considered the most vulnerable court to attack. Both sides of the court will be protected on the outside sections where the players can be pulled wide to return serve. The left-handed player positioned in the left area provides the same protection as the better backhand in that position. When the strongest player is positioned on the right side of the court, the tactic switches dramatically. Support for this alignment is centered on the fact that more serves are hit to the right service court than the left in every match, and the stronger player would be positioned to return more serves than the weaker player. In addition, the server has a better angle to place serves to left and right corners of the right service court (assuming the server is right-handed), which permits the talents of the stronger player to be used more effectively. The left service court is left open to mostly wide backhand returns for a right-handed player who, with practice, can develop a skill at returning that one basic shot.

Regardless of the final decision, there is a crucial alignment that must be considered if the team is to receive serve correctly, and if the serving team is going to serve from the correct positions. The receiving partner follows the division line theory in aligning with the server's position, and in moving up or back in relation to the baseline, adjusting to the speed and spin of the service. The receiving partner begins at the back of the opposite service court line halfway between the singles sideline and the division of the service court line. The serving team's server stands approximately halfway between the singles sideline and the center mark, while the server's net partner is positioned in the middle of the opposite service court. Reactions of all four players following serve relate to doubles play entirely. The receiver returns the serve and makes a decision to advance to the net or stay at the baseline until the receiving team has gained an advantage and the player can go to the net. The receiving partner moves toward the net following serve

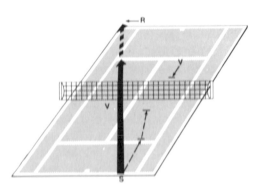

Serving and Moving to the Net in Doubles

until positioned a racket and a half away from the net (as skill increases, the closeness to the net is diminished). The server follows the serve to the net, remembering to stop before the ball crosses the net, then continues the advance once the ball is returned by the serving team. The following of the serve to the net should not be taken as literally in doubles play as in singles play. The server actually goes straight forward to a net position. The serving partner at the net simply closes on the net, as does the receiving partner.

The decision on *which partner begins serve* is simple if ego is eliminated. The partner who has the more consistent serve and who possesses a strong spin serve should begin each set. Taking advantage of consistency is imperative to success at doubles, because it gives the serving team the advantage at the net — and controlling the net is correlated with winning. A team given a choice of serve or receive at the beginning of the match should elect to serve for the same reasons that the stronger server serves first in a set.

Communication is indispensable to a cohesive partnership in doubles. There are three ways to communicate: 1) one-word directions, 2) signals, and 3) body language and/or intuition.

One-word communication consists of "mine" and "yours" for who returns a shot, and "up" or "back" for moving to the net or retreating from the net as a team. Two additional commands are "bounce it" and "out." "Bounce it" means that the ball is close to the line and that it is best to let it bounce before hitting it. It is advisable that the call for "bounce it" should be made when the player can still hit the ball following its bounce. The term "out" is an obvious call that the ball is definitely going to land out of bounds and should not be returned or hit in any manner.

Communication by *hand signals* is done prior to a serve. The serving team signals to indicate player movement, location of the serve, type of serve, and poaching. The signals are given from the net by the net partner using either a closed fist, open hand, or a combination of fingers. The receiving team on occasion also gives signals, particularly when attacking an Australian doubles team formation. Teams that are advanced in skill often depend on signals, while less experienced teams may consult through conversation before receiving or serving.

Signals

The last form of communication is *body language or intuition.* Players who have played together for a long time, or who are highly compatible, will tend to combine body language and intuition with the other two forms of communication.

A final consideration is verbal discussion before a match to determine who will hit returns of balls down the middle, and to determine or review the game plan. Communication must take place for a successful team effort, and to avoid mistakes of court position.

SERVICE AND RETURN OF SERVICE STRATEGY

The first service in doubles is of extreme importance. Three-fourths of all first serves should be hit successfully to give the serving team the leverage of moving to the net as a team in a two up volley situation. Once the developing player has progressed beyond hitting flat services with pace to areas of the opponents' service courts, spin serves should be used in the majority of situations.

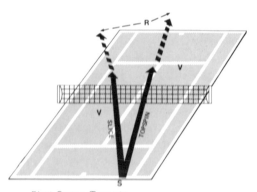

First Serve Targets

Topspin serves should be hit to the backhand of the receiver as a first serve, forcing the return of serve to be high at the net and pushing the receiver back a little more than normal to prevent a strong advance on the net from the receiver's position. As a variation, a slice serve should be used when serving to the opposing team's right service court to force the receiver off the court, and to allow the attacking serving team to overplay to their left to·control the net. To reiterate, the service must be consistently accurate, and the placement, with spin, must be thoughtfully considered. Additionally, the beginner must work hard at protecting the partner at the net during service. A soft, pushed serve will endanger that partner and compel the team to play two back on serve, thus defeating the advantage of controlling the net by the serving team.

There are two considerations attached to a *return of service* in doubles: first, to get the ball back over the net at the serving team's feet; second, to select the best target placement of the return, and then complete that task. The first consideration is an obvious strategy related to self-preservation that has to be the prerequisite with no exceptions. The second consideration requires more planning and assessment of at least four options for target areas:

1. Return the ball to the feet of the net player or the advancing server.
2. Pass the net player.
3. Lob the net player.
4. Hit cross-court angled toward the server.

The first three options were discussed in an earlier chapter as they related to playing a net player. With a service return, lobbing becomes difficult with a serve of any pace, but it is reasonably effective off a soft serve. If the net player does not advance on the net to within a two steps from net position, the return at the net player can be effective also. Passing the net player requires that the player at the net lean to the middle with the anticipation of poaching, and the return is directed toward the alley. Being able to pass an opponent at the net down the alley is a demoralizing act, since that is the one area the net player must protect. The angled cross-court returns and cross-court returns at the onrushing server's feet are exceptional for hitting winning shots. Angled cross-court shots cannot be reached by the server unless the server anticipates the shot, or the angled return lacks crispness. Cross-

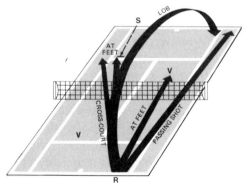

Return of Service in Doubles Options

court shots at the feet of the server moving to the net catch the server in a tentative position, and the final result is often a ball hit up for an easy volley by the receiving team. The choice of which return to hit is to a large extent controlled by the placement of the serve in the service court, and by the velocity of the serve. A serve hit to the inside corner of the right service court usually eliminates the passing shot at the net player due to the central location of the ball. All other service returns from that location remain possible, with the best choice a return at the attacking server's feet. A serve placement to the inside of the left service court has the same response as the serve to the inside of the right service court. Serves hit wide to the respective service courts permit all four service return options to be used. The major lesson to be learned is that a good server will only give the receiver a limited number of options to select from during any given service situation. If a serve is well placed, the receiver will return serve to anticipated areas on the serving team's side of the court. One last consideration of return of serve is for the receiving player to always get the racket on the ball. All strategy for a return of serve collapses if the receiver misses the return.

NET PLAY STRATEGY

Net play is divided between the serving and receiving team's reactions. The *server's role* is to serve an accurate serve, then move to a net position. The server should follow a path straight to the net midway between the singles sideline and the midline of the service courts. The server must stop prior to the ball crossing the net, and after the serving team hits their first return in the rally, the server moves forward again, finally closing in on the net. All volleys hit by the *serving team* must place pressure on the receiving team through depth, firmness of the stroke, and low trajectory. The *server's partner* must protect the alley and poach under certain conditions. The serving team is the aggressor, and it has to force the play on the receiving team.

The *receiving team's* early goal is to drive the serving team away from the net. The *receiver of serve* stays at the baseline until an advantage can be taken, then advances to the net to support the partner. There are times when the receiver will immediately move to the net (besides the following of a strong return by the receiving team), but a weakness is also exposed when the receiver attacks without protection. The *receiver's partner* is in a precarious position when being forced to react to whatever shot return the serving team can devise. This position is a basically defensive one until an advantage can be gained by the receiving team. The receiving partner also must protect the alley and poach when circumstances are acceptable.

When all four players are at the net attacking each other, the play is extremely fun. When a ball is hit at a player, that player must react by using the racket as an involuntary reflex reaction to the ball. Most volley returns are from the backhand side if a ball is hit directly at a player. Players become acclimated to the blocking of a ball from the backhand side. Therefore, a good strategy is to create a problem for a net player by hitting at the forehand side to force the player to react a second time from the learned reaction of leaning to the backhand. Hitting the ball at the feet of the opponent in a face-to-face volley causes the return to be hit "up," which means that the team faced with an "up" ball can hit "down." To hit a volley "down" is a decided advantage for that team. Another reaction for a four up situation is for one team to lift a volley lob over the opposing team, chasing them back to the baseline. All three suggestions for strategy when all four players are at the net are a step beyond what the early beginner would be able to achieve, but with a little experience at the net, the strategy will begin to develop in a logical sequence.

THE AIR GAME AND IT'S STRATEGY

The air game is a concept of the air being filled with tennis balls via lobs and overheads. That concept occurs extensively in doubles play. A player at the net must always be ready for a lob, since that is a significant means of attacking a net player or a team at the net.

The response to a lob is an *overhead*, and any ball hit between the net and the service court backline is an automatic overhead if the ball is higher than the racket when the player settles under the ball. The targets provided through the angled overheads and deep overheads were discussed in the chapter on singles strategy, and those targets hold true with doubles play. The position of the opposing team that has lobbed has much to do with final placement of an overhead smash. If both players are back, an angled overhead is most appropriate. If both players are up, they had better duck, because the overhead should be directed at their bodies or feet. If confronted with a one up — one back formation — the overhead should either be directed at the player at the net, or hit between the two players. As with the volley tandem movement, a team anticipating an overhead should move together as a tandem. If a smash has been hit to the opponent's right side of the court, the movement of the team should be to the left, splitting the division line with one player on each side. The imaginary line between the partners should be at a right angle to the division line. This movement will leave a small portion of the right side open for the team returning the overhead, but a return off an overhead would be an exceptional shot if hit to that area. The tandem movement fits both volley and overhead smash reaction to the ball and it follows a basic premise of a balanced court coverage.

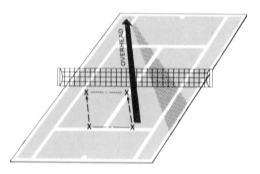

Tandem Doubles Movement to Hit Overhead Smashes and Volleys

Returning a *lob* is a part of all doubles strategy, and it is simple if the players have the skill to hit a lob. Defensive lobs are designed to drive a team at the net back when the lobbing team is attempting to recover from an excellent offensive attack. Offensive lobs are hit when the lobbing team has control of the baseline and doesn't have to move extensively to get to the ball. The offensive lob not only drives the opposing team back, but it permits the lobbing team to take control of the net. The lob game is one of attacking, retreating, and attacking again. If a good offensive lob can cause a weak return of a short return lob, the set up is available for an overhead smash from the net position.

THE DOUBLES GAMES PLAN AND STRATEGY

The doubles plan of strategy is to execute strokes in an attacking manner, working to gain control of the net. All players at all levels of skill must do those two things. One of the easier skills in tennis is the volley shot. If a beginner can get to the net, play will be highly enjoyable from that position. Once the concept of taking control of the net is ingrained, the doubles team must remember to protect the alley and middle of the court. They must learn to move as a team, in a tandem, supporting each other and retreating or advancing together. The receiving team must return serves on a low trajectory with pace and attempt to hit a predetermined target area. The serving team needs to establish a relentless plan of attack with the server coming to the net following a well-placed serve. The final plan is to communicate with the partner, out-think the opposing team, and out-react the opponent.

Chapter Twelve

Drills For The
Developing Tennis Player

Practice in between playing matches is good combination for developing tennis skills and then applying them. Any group instruction class has numerous drills that are used each class period to develop skill. Hopefully, reinforcement comes from playing in class and from suggestions during the performance of each drill and play situation. The developing tennis player needs more work than can be provided in a group instruction situation, however, and that work or practice can be achieved in additional practice time with two types of drills. One type is described as "tennis by yourself," a series of drills for the individual player where no partner is needed. The second type is termed "tennis with a partner" where a partner is needed for practice who is either more skilled or as skilled as the developing player.

TENNIS BY YOURSELF

"Tennis by yourself" involves drills that require no partner, develop strokes with a checkpoint of mechanics reminders, and encourage variation in the drill selection. There are many occasions when a player cannot find a suitable partner or one who wants to practice. The drills presented below will take 45 minutes and will give the developing player a good physical workout plus a skill practice session that requires only one participant.

The *serving* practice drill requires a player to use thirty tennis balls in serving to targets. The level of skill will establish the type of serves hit, and through a series of six sets, a player will hit 180 tennis serves.

Set #1: Serve 30 balls to the left service court — inside corner.
Set #2: Serve 30 balls to the right service court — inside corner.
Set #3: Serve 30 balls to the left service court — outside corner.

Set #4: Serve 30 balls to the right service court — outside corner.

Set #5: Serve 30 balls to the left service court — 10 to the outside, 10 to the middle, 10 to the inside.

Set #6: Serve 30 balls to the right service court — 10 to the outside, 10 to the middle, 10 to the inside.

Movement Requirement: player must run to the other side of the court and retrieve balls in a pickup run fashion.

Checkpoint of Mechanics: Counting successful serves might be insightful, but total concentration on mechanics will be more productive.

1. Am I looking at the tennis ball on the toss?
2. Is my toss accurate? high enough? in line?
3. Are my feet where they belong?
4. Do I have a full back swing? follow through?
5. Is my grip appropriate to my serve?
6. Am I accurate? why? why not?

Variations: Variations are quite acceptable, but only one type of serve per set should be initiated. A good variation is to serve and to go to the net for a volley, stopping as the ball strikes the service court.

The second drill — a simple *groundstroke* — uses a wall board, but goals must be set through the sequence. There are nine sets in the drill lasting sixty seconds each. After each stroke, the player must return to ready position and allow a distance to permit the ball to bounce twice before each stroke.

Set #1: Hit repetitive forehands.

Set #2: Hit repetitive backhands (remember to drop on the backhand side).

Set #3: Alternate forehand and backhand.

Sets #4, 5, and 6: Repeat sets 1-3 with slice.

Sets #7, 8, and 9: Repeat sets 1-3 with topspin.

Checkpoints of Mechanics:
1. Am I looking the ball into the racket?
2. Am I transferring weight into the ball?
3. Do I have a full back swing? follow through?
4. Am I hitting with the appropriate grip?
5. Am I turning my shoulder early?
6. Is the ball at least 5' high on the wall board?
7. Am I accurate? why? why not?

The third drill is designed to develop confidence and eliminate overanxiety in players hitting *approach shots*. Approach shots are seldom executed in practice, so hitting four sets of thirty balls each will provide a good mental inset. Aim at the service court line for depth and 4' in from the sideline for accuracy. The player should drop the balls at least 2 feet away and at least waist high.

Set #1: From middle of the right service court, hit forehand slice down the line.

Set #2: From middle of the left service court, hit backhand slice down the line.

Set #3: From middle of the right service court, hit forehand topspin cross-court.

Set #4: From middle of the left service court, hit backhand topspin cross-court.

Movement Requirements: player must run to the other side of the court and retrieve balls in a pickup run fashion.

Checkpoints of Mechanics:
1. Am I letting the ball drop, and am I timing my strokes?
2. Am I looking the ball into my racket?
3. Am I transferring my weight?
4. Is my backswing shortened?
5. Am I hitting into the court? why? why not?

Variations: The type of shot can be varied. For the player who hasn't developed slice or topspin, a basic flat stroke can be substituted. Hitting topspin down the line is another variation of the drill. Also, placing the ball on the drop in different areas of the service court and between the baseline and the service court line contributes to variation.

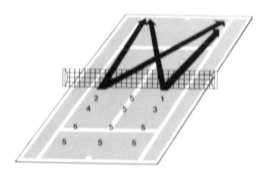

Approach Shot Movement Drill

Moving is a prime need for a tennis player. Coupled with agility and quickness, movement can aid the player in getting to the ball in time. Three sets are designed to encourage agility and quickness and use of the racket in shadow boxing.

Set #1: The player should move to imaginary numbers and, in sequence, shadow box either a groundstroke, approach shot, or volley. All balls stroked up to the service line require the players to return to ready position on the baseline, and all balls between the service line and the net require the player to assume a ready position at the net in the middle.

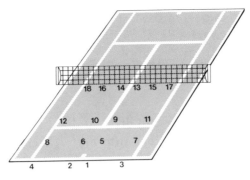

Shadow Boxing Movement Drill #1

Set #2: The same drill as above except the shadow boxing should consist of lobs from the baseline and overhead smashes from the net. Player must assume ready position on each stroke.

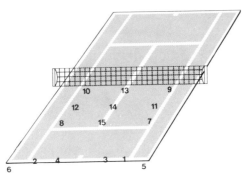

Shadow Boxing Movement Drill #2

Set #3: The player eliminates shadow boxing and moves along the lines of the court, touching each junction between two lines.

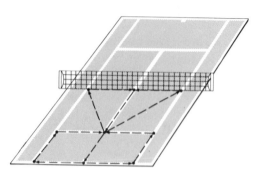

Fitness Movement Drill

The final drill is an *overhead smash*. The exercise requires a simple bounce of the ball off the court and above the head, providing time for the player to get set underneath the ball and hit an overhead smash.

Set #1: Hit 15 overheads from the right middle service court.

Set #2: Hit 15 overheads from the left middle service court.

Set #3: Hit 15 overheads from the right center position halfway between baseline and service line.

Set #4: Hit 15 overheads from the left center position halfway between baseline and service line.

Movement Requirement: After each pair of sets, the player must run to the other side of the court and retrieve balls in a pickup fashion.

Checkpoint of Mechanics:
1. Am I timing my stroke in a smooth, rhythmical motion?
2. Is my backswing in the middle of my shoulder blades and my elbow up at a right angle?
3. Do I have my non-racket hand pointing in reference to the ball?
4. Am I hitting into the court? why? why not?

Variations: The player may locate other posts to hit the overhead and begin to identify the location of the target on the other side of the court.

There are numerous sets for each skill and other skills that can be developed. The key to executing the drills is having a little self-discipline, becoming goal oriented, and building confidence that each skill can be performed. If the developing player will participate three times per week in "tennis by yourself," a marked change in skill development will occur.

PARTNER PRACTICE

It is imperative that a developing player find a reliable practice partner. However, if the partner is only available on occasion, then three or four practice partners might be in order. There are literally thousands of drills for practice and skill development; the developing player needs only a few good ones.

Baseline drills, if goal oriented, can be of great value. Five drills that enhance skill are outlined below. The drills focus on particular parts of a baseline rally with emphasis on percentage tennis.

Hitting *cross-court* is a simple rally that involves hitting only forehand for an extended period of time, then hitting backhand for the same length of time. The balls should be hit between the service line and baseline, and to the extreme of center. The player's home base is a long step from the center mark, with the player returning to that spot after each stroke and assuming a ready position.

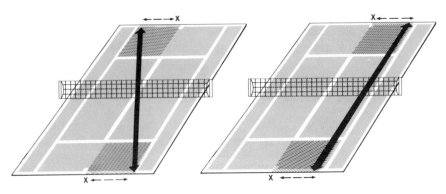

Hitting Cross-Court Drill   *Hitting Down the Sideline Drill*

Hitting *down the sideline* is an extension of the cross-court rally except that the partners rally down the right sideline for an extended period of time, then switch to the left sideline. One player hits a forehand groundstroke, while the other hits a backhand. As with the cross-court drill, the players must return after each stroke to a ready position within a step of the center mark. Each ball should be hit between the baseline and service line, and to the extreme of center.

A *combination of down the line and cross-court* drills incorporates a nice movement with the imprinting of two basic directions for strokes. The idea is for one player to hit only cross-court while the other player hits only down the line. Each stroke requires the players to return to center in a ready position. Given a time frame, the partners switch roles. Again, each ball must be hit between the service court line and the baseline. A suggestion for all three drills is to stop play when control is lost and restart the drill. Another suggestion is to use all three groundstrokes: topspin cross-court and down the line, slice down the line, and basic groundstroke cross-court and down the line.

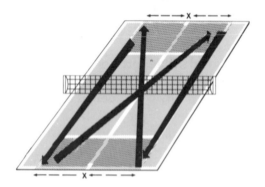

Combination Down the Line — Cross-Court Drill

The fourth baseline drill is a competitive one that forces the ball to be hit deep between the service court line and the baseline. The game is called 21 and consists of a drop hit followed by a rally. The first person to hit short (between the service line and net) or err in stroke play (i.e., hit the net, hit out of bounds, etc.) loses a point. The first player to 21 wins the game. The play should respond to baseline court strategy, moving the partner, setting up a shot, and, most important, hitting deep.

The last baseline drill — the *bounce-hit*, is a concentration drill that forces the partners to focus on the ball. Following the drop to start a rally, both players verbalize the word "bounce" every time the ball bounces on the court, and when the ball is stroked, both players state "hit." Initially the partners will feel self-conscious and attempt to disregard the drill as a silly exercise. But given two minutes, the efficiency of making good mechanical contact and the consistency of the ball going back across the net will convince nearly every skeptic that there is something to the drill. The "something" is the forced focus on the ball and the subsequent blocking of all distractions, plus the elimination of all thinking except for the use of the words "bounce" and "hit."

Serve and return drills enable partners to practice two skills at one time. The server can work on various serves while the receiver can first concentrate on blocking returns and second on returning to target areas. There are vulnerable service targets that a server wants to be able to hit and that a receiver needs to be able to develop confidence in returning. The partners should use a bag of balls on this drill. The targets for the server are the left and right inside and outside corners of both service courts, and the outside edge of each court. The receiver with prior knowledge of the location works on rotating shoulders from a ready position and blocking the returns back deep. Given a period of time on this sequence, the receiving partner with experience begins to stroke each return to designated target areas. Outside corners are re-turned cross-court, and inside corners are returned deep back to the server. When the server has the skill to hit slice and topspin service, those serves should be hit in a repetitive order, and the receiver should again look for the target areas and return serves to those areas. As can be observed, there are numerous variations of this drill, and players should be innovative and design what helps them individually. Standardized drills are not a necessity if the developing player has any imagination.

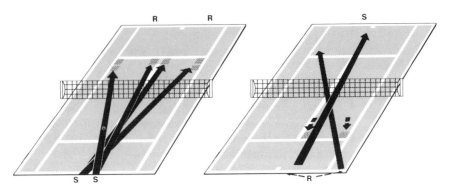

Serve and Return Target Drill # 1   Serve and Return Target Drill # 2

Serve and volley drills can be of immeasurable fun and work. One helpful drill requires the server to serve to approved target areas and then proceed to the net for volley shots. The receiver has a dual role of returning serve and providing set up volley shots for the server. The server hits the first serve and advances to the service court line for the first volley. The receiver, with three tennis balls in hand, returns the serve at the service court line. If the receiver is erratic at the service return and subsequent volley situations, the tennis balls are dropped and hit to the server. The server, following the first volley, proceeds across the service court line, stops, and then returns the second volley. Finally, the server advances to within two steps of the net and punches the last volley, following the same stopping procedure prior to hitting the ball. There are several keys to the drill. The server must learn to stop and then begin to transfer weight into each volley. Second, the partner has to synchronize each drop hit to simulate normal play. Third, the server, in attacking the net, has to be aware of position and hit volleys deep or cross-court.

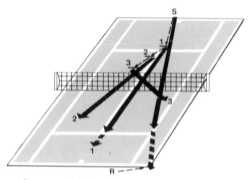

Serve and Volley Drill

Combining *groundstrokes and volleying* helps both partners develop skills simultaneously. The groundstroke partner drop hits a forehand groundstroke down the line to the volleyer, who punches a volley back to the partner's forehand. That sequence is repeated and then changed to a groundstroke down the line and forehand volley return to the backhand. The drill can continue with groundstrokes hit as cross-court and returned as cross-court at the net —first with forehands and then with backhands. The target in both

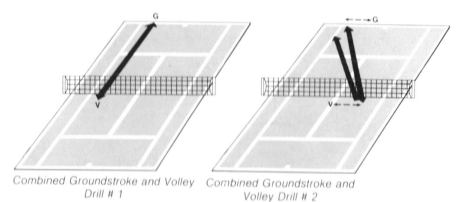

Combined Groundstroke and Volley   *Combined Groundstroke and*
Drill # 1   *Volley Drill # 2*

drills for the volleying partner is to hit deep and to go to the side identified. One volley drill that is enormous fun and yet instructional, tests reflexes. Both partners begin the drill at mid-baseline service court line, and volley moving toward each other. The volleys can begin forehand to forehand, then proceed backhand to backhand, and then alternate. The *workup volley* drill enhances "seeing" the ball, reflexes, and form. The idea is to return each shot to the partner and advance.

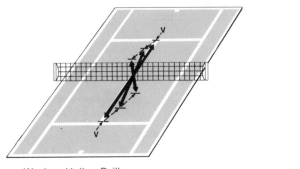

Workup Volley Drill

Another combination drill is the *Groundstroke-Volley-Lob-Overhead*. The baseline partner hits a groundstroke that the net partner volleys deep center. The next shot is a mid-court lob, with the net partner retrieving and hitting an overhead to deep center. The drill continues with a groundstroke-volley combination, a lob-overhead combination, etc. The targets can change with both partners. Groundstrokes can be directed to the forehand of the net player and returned cross-court, or to the backhand and returned cross-court. The possibilities are endless, and the partners will find themselves saying, "Let's try . . . ."

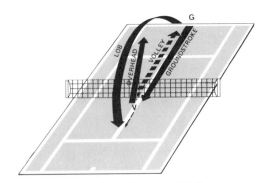

Groundstroke, Volley, Lob, Overhead Drill

Lobs and overheads go together like bread and butter. The partners in this drill have to alternate lobs and overheads. The drill begins with one partner at the baseline and one at the net. The baseline partner (partner A) hits a lob to the mid-court area of partner B that requires partner B to step back, hit an overhead smash, and return to the net. Partner A must then hit a deep lob to the baseline of partner B, forcing partner B to retreat all the way to the baseline to return a short lob to the mid-court area of Partner A. Partner A, following the deep lob, is required to move to the net, then retreat to hit the mid-court lob of Partner B. The sequence continues throughout the drill with an imaginary string attached to both partners that limits their movement to two-thirds of the court. One partner is always at the net, and one always at the baseline. This lob-overhead drill continues until the fatigue becomes too great. This excellent drill encourages position play. The nice thing about the drill is if the depth of the lob or overhead is missed, the situation is repeated until the partners get back in synchronization. If the partners can remember that they are on a string, they will develop the idea that each has to move in line with the other. An easier drill that encourages accuracy of lobs simply

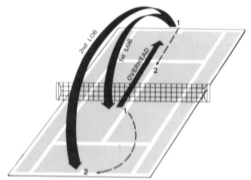

Alternating Lob Overhead Drill

requires that each partner lob to the other. The drill becomes more of a challenge if targets are set. Hitting cross-court lobs that one player hits as a defensive lob, and the other hits offensively is one variation. Rallying and hitting moonballs is a second variation.

Drills can be extremely simple or quite complex. The developing player needs to progress from the simple to the complex. Working with drills in a practice session can be enjoyable if skills are combined into drills, if drills are challenging, and if the partners use their imagination to devise new drills.

Chapter Thirteen

Mental Aspects of Tennis Competition

It obviously takes physical effort and mental planning of strategy to be successful in tennis. Without the physical skill, an individual would have a very difficult time winning. The mental state, however, goes beyond physical skill — it actually replenishes the physical effort. The mental effort that controls the tennis match is the intangible that accents the physical and gives direction to the purpose of playing tennis. The mental aspects of tennis are the true key to success on a tennis court.

A developing tennis player should ask "Why participate in a game that requires so much from a player, both physically and mentally?" To play tennis requires a bit of a childlike personality. The player has to want to play for play's sake. Associated with that concept is the acceptance of playing for fun and for the sheer joy of physical movement and abandonment. The tennis player needs to feel the game, feel the esthetics, and appreciate the execution of skill. Playing for fitness or even skill development, and played for fun, contribute to the special feeling of participating in tennis for the right reasons. A player should feel the sun and breeze caressing the body and absorb the sound of balls striking rackets, the chatter of people, and the sounds of effort as a player reaches for an overhead. If the game is played for the correct reasons, all the other parts, including winning, fall into place.

UNDERSTANDING WHAT COMPETITION REALLY MEANS

Competition and winning are often confused as being the same, but they are barely related. In competition, winning is a by-product for at least one of the participants. Competition is not opponent against opponent — it is player against barrier. If the tennis player can visualize that the player on the other side of the net is placing barriers, an understanding of competition begins to emerge. The opponent — through a serve, a volley, or a lob — is placing a barrier for the other player to respond to in an effective manner. The barrier is placed in front of a player for a challenge. It is nothing personal, and a tennis player must see that to be really successful in a match, and to learn to truly compete.

A developing player must learn to emphasize *execution over winning*. If execution is the important aspect, the winning will take care of itself. Worrying about winning or losing interferes with both execution and winning. Thinking about appearance or pleasing others interferes with execution and winning. The emphasis is on execution, the concentration is on execution, and the goal is execution. A clarification is in order when the term "execution" is used. The emphasis is not on thinking about executing a skill pattern — it is on completing the skill pattern. The mind should be focused on feeling a barrier and responding to it by a reflex action, and that reflex action is execution. If a player begins to analyze movement and strokes, or begins to think of ulterior motives behind execution, there is a collapse of skilled play. The developing tennis player may never have been exposed to this concept before and so may have difficulty understanding why thinking about winning is not acceptable. If the player will realize that emphasis on winning places pressure to excel and pressure to not fail, then the idea of eliminating those pressures might become palatable. If executing by doing provides the realization of the long-term goal of winning, then execution begins to make sense.

ELIMINATING NEGATIVE ATTITUDES

A *negative attitude or negative feelings* contribute to a negative response when participating in tennis. If a developing player is ready to receive a serve and the thought "please don't make the serve; double fault — please" flashes, a very negative attitude has been established. Other thoughts that seem to be a part of the game include "what if I miss the shot," or "if I hold my serve I can win," or "you dummy — why can't you hit the ball?" Each thought plants a seed of negative response that contributes to a less than successful experience. Negative attitudes arise when a player gets upset and begins to talk to the other self: "how could you hit such a stupid shot" or "I can't believe you are real — how could you miss such an easy set up?" If a player keeps making derogatory statements about performance, that player will exceed all expectations of failure through negative thought. *Fear of winning and fear of losing* are both contributing factors to negative thought. Fear places pressure on the player to not make mistakes, and that negative reemphasizes fear of failure. The player becomes anxious to do well, and that anxiousness contributes to tension, which restricts performance (since performance must be accomplished in a relaxed, controlled manner).

Becoming *angry and losing one's temper* is another negative. The anger is a means of releasing energy, and this will take a toll on the player when a demand for extra effort is needed and the body cannot provide it. Losing temper also places pressure on that player. A player who gets mad at himself or herself is venting anger internally. That internal anger creates the same anxiety as when there is a fear of winning or losing, with the player trying to please "self." The effect of the cycle of anger-anxiety-pressure is the collapse of the player's performance during competition.

Another negative associated with performance and tennis play is the behavior of the opponent. There is a very popular term in sport — *psyching out.*" Behavior by an opponent can be upsetting if permitted to be upsetting. Body language, verbal comments, gamesmanship, and outbursts by an opponent can create negative reactions that will create anxiety for the other player. The feeling of "why did she say that" or "I wish he would shut his mouth" establish negative thought patterns in the other player.

Negative thoughts can be changed by realizing what is happening and replacing them with positive thoughts. Instead of worrying about a missed shot, concentration should focus on remembering a similar shot that was executed well. Instead of hoping that an opponent will miss a serve, a player should demand that the serve be good so that "I can have the opportunity to return a winner." The fear of winning and/or losing is eliminated if the player will remember and practice what competition means and will shut out the emphasis on winning and losing. Certainly attacking one's own person verbally and sometimes physically is not being a friend to the inner self. The developing player should treat the inner self with respect and dignity, stop arguing with and embarrassing one's other self, and begin to compliment the other self on a good shot or a good point played. Finally, not allowing an opponent to apply psyching techniques is extremely helpful in facing competition.

CONCENTRATION

Concentration is a very important part of tennis. Blocking out all factors other than executing a shot is required to have good concentration and ultimate success. Concentration is centered around *focus*. The focus on the ball and the task of hitting the ball, along with the focus on the environment, helps a player to concentrate. When engaged in a rally, the player should look at the seams of the ball all the way to the racket face. Research indicates that a player can only see a ball to within four feet of the racket, but just the effort to look the ball into the racket improves concentration. During a rally, the player should use the drill "bounce-hit" as a means of concentration. There is a restriction on verbalizing the words bounce and hit out loud, but the mental tabulation of bounce and hit would serve a useful purpose. Concentration is also enhanced by certain environmental situations. One of those is being in touch with one's own body. The ability to synchronize breathing with each stroke, and sensing the heartbeat as a body function, permit the player to be in touch. Other senses also enhance concentration, including hearing the tennis ball make contact with the racket strings, feeling the impact of ball and racket, and recognizing muscle contraction and tension during the stroke. To really concentrate requires an elimination of all extraneous aspects of the environment. Exchanging sides of the court is a time for concentration and relaxing. The concentration should be on the extension of the game plan and thinking positive thoughts. If a player keeps saying "I am playing well," after awhile that thought becomes reality. Concentration is focusing on the task at hand.

ANXIETY AND SLUMPS

There will be times when everything "clicks" during a game, and there will be a *flow* to movement and to the play in general. That flow may last for a few points in a match, for a larger portion of a match, for a few days, or for months. Then there will be down times, situations where nothing seems to work and where Murphy's Law is for real. The down time is described best as a *slump*, and a slump is caused by *anxiety*. Slumps seem to appear for no reason, but they usually are a result of worrying, tension, or a fear of winning/losing. In short, slumps occur as a result of pressure that is self-induced, and that pressure causes anxiety. Once a player becomes anxious, muscles tense, which, in turn, forces physical errors, since there is no relaxation during stroke execution. When the errors mount, tension increases and the slump continues. As long as the player permits the pressure to interfere with performance the cycle will continue.

The cure to the slump is to eliminate the anxiety by reducing muscle tension. This can be done in two ways: 1) the player begins to cope with success and failure and begins to think positive, and 2) the player begins to relax and hit out on each ball, eliminating concern for end result. In order to reduce muscle tension, the player needs to rebuild confidence. Participating in a match with a player who hits with consistent pace is a start at redeveloping that confidence, and self-talks, including "good shot — way to play," aid in raising the self-esteem necessary for self-confidence. Believing that the flow will return and relaxing are keys to coping in a positive manner. As a means of relaxing, the player must work at minimizing the number of times the muscle groups will be permitted to tense, thus decreasing interference with relaxed performance. During competition when the flow is present, it often disappears when the player realizes that "I shouldn't be playing this well." There is a self-fulfilling prophecy that begins to make the player anxious, and the whole cycle within the match begins to develop. An interesting aspect of the prophecy is that in the next match a slump may not be evident, but somewhere in the match, if similar circumstances occur, play will deteriorate just as before. Regardless of the length of the slump, the anxiety causes muscle tension, which reduces performance.

THE CONTRIBUTION OF RELAXATION

The ability to relax contributes greatly to physical performance. Learning how to relax in a tennis match is related to recognizing muscle tension. If the player grips the racket with excessive force (an exception when hitting volley shots), muscle tension is too great. Shoulder and arm muscles that are tight can be recognized with a little practice. Tenseness in the mouth and jaw areas is a common occurrence, and a check of the jaw will reveal this. The whole body can tense during the pressure of a particular point or game, and shortness of breath, excessive sweating, and mental confusion are signals that the stress is too great. Relaxation during play can be attained in several ways: 1) by immediately responding to tension on the court, 2) by preparing to play through mental rehearsal and mental imagery, and 3) by relaxing before the match.

The *immediate response to tension on the court* is to learn how to recognize the tension and then relax those muscle groups. If the player feels tension in the shoulders and neck, a clockwise rotation of the head followed by a counterclockwise motion will relax that area. Tension in the arms and legs can be eliminated by running or skipping in place. Another exercise that aids in total body relaxation is to take a deep breath and hold for a count of five, finally expelling the air.

Preparing to play through the use of *mental rehearsal or mental imagery* requires practice, but it can be learned in a short time. The idea is to prepare so well mentally that confidence is enhanced, which, in turn, reduces anxiety and tension. There are several approaches to this way of developing relaxation. One is to correct a skill problem by visualizing the mistake, then repeatedly reviewing the proper skill with the mind. Sometimes the skill problem is more related to the sequence of shots or a game plan, and the corresponding mental practice should be to use imagery emphasizing the acceptable shot or sequence of shots in a game plan. This mental imagery is a foundation for the actual tennis match and will assist the player in recognizing certain situations. Mental rehearsal even helps during a match when a player visualizes a positive picture of the next sequence of serves or a strategy for moving the ball from one side of the court to the other in a baseline rally.

The third form of relaxation is *pre-match relaxation*. The most widely used technique is *progressive relaxation*, which involves developing a habitual twenty-minute-per-day relaxation exercise plus a before-a-match session. Skill development is centered on recognizing muscle tension followed by relaxing each muscle group (see Table 13.0). The tension recognition and relaxation response provides a foundation to approach both life and tennis on a more relaxed level. This skill carries over to a tennis match by permitting the player to recognize pressure during play, and immediately relaxing enough to prevent a deterioration of performance. Other forms of pre-match relaxation include meditation and self-hypnosis, and are all compatible for use by a tennis player to improve performance. The progressive relaxation technique and additional forms of pre-match relaxation also contribute to the player using mental rehearsal or imagery after attaining a position of relaxation.

The mental aspects of tennis preparation can raise the level of a player's skill to an optimum not considered possible. The game is more mental than physical. The developing player must make the effort to understand what competition really is, and apply that knowledge in play. If negative thoughts can be eliminated and anxiety reduced, play will improve. If concentration is developed, and various forms of relaxation are applied, the player will improve rapidly. Mental aspects of tennis require that the player change former attitudes of competition, and apply the mental to the physical effort in a positive manner. The mental aspect of tennis is a psychological and philosophical approach to playing the game, and to enjoying life through tennis.

Table 13.0
Recognition of Muscle Tension and Relaxation
of the Various Muscle Groups

Tense in Order the Following Muscle Groups	After Each Tensing of a Muscle Group Relax That Muscle Group
1. Tense lower arm, wrist, and hand by tightening muscles in each area — right side.	1. Slowly relax each muscle area beginning with the lower arm, and progressing to the hand — right side.
2. Tense the upper arm and elbow by tightening each muscle group — right side.	2. Slowly relax the upper arm and elbow — right side.
3. Shrug the right shoulder touching the right ear. Repeat on the left shoulder.	3. Relax the shoulder.
4. Repeat numbers 1 and 2 on the left side.	4. Repeat the relaxation of numbers 1 and 2.
5. Tense the lower leg, ankle, and foot by tightening the muscles in each area — right side.	5. Slowly relax each muscle area beginning with the lower leg, and progressing to the foot — right side.
6. Tense the upper leg; the hamstring separately from the quadricep, if possible — right side.	6. Slowly relax the upper leg — right side.
7. Repeat numbers 5 and 6 on the left side.	7. Repeat the relaxation of number 5 and 6.
8. Tense the following face muscles: a. Tighten the jaw by clenching the teeth. b. Press the tongue against the roof of the mouth. c. Pucker the lips and hold. d. Wrinkle the brow.	a. Relax the jaw by laying the head back. b. Relax the lower jaw by returning the tongue to the normal position. c. Relax the lips. d. Relax by stopping the wrinkling of the brow.

Note: 1. Repeat each number twice before proceeding on to the next sequence.
2. Each exercise should last for a minimum of five seconds.
3. When the exercises have been completed, place a scene of a blue sky with blue water and warm breezes into an imagery pattern for 20 minutes.

Chapter Fourteen

The Tennis Court and the Equipment Design

Tennis courts, rackets, balls, and clothing have evolved over the years and gained considerable sophistication. To be informed, the developing player should have some basic knowledge of tennis courts and equipment.

THE TENNIS COURT

There are five categories of *tennis court surfaces*. *Grass courts* are traditional but have outlived their usefulness. The Wimbledon and Australian Open are still played on a grass court, but the upkeep and expense involved in maintaining the surface are nearly prohibitive. There are few grass courts in the United States, and they are nearly extinct worldwide. Soft courts are popular throughout much of the world and east of the Mississippi River in the United States. The typical soft court is a *clay court*, and its surface provides a high bounce and a slow ball that encourage long baseline rallys. The term "clay court" is descriptive of the surface, composed of a claylike material and coarse sand. The clay surface poses a maintenance problem when reasonable play conditions are desired, because it requires extensive watering and rolling.

The *all-weather or hard court* surfaces are extremely popular in the United States. This is the surface with which most developing players are familiar. The surface may be composed of asphalt or cement topping, which contributes to ease of maintenance and cleaning. Courts with this surface are usually public, and they are easily recognized because they provide a uniform, fast-bouncing action to the ball. The *synthetic surface*, is another type of hard surface that has been used by many developing players on their college campuses. The synthetic court surface is usually composed of a series of granulated rubber particles pulled together with an epoxy resin sprayed with a polyurethane coating and laid on a porous foundation. The court is designed to play like a naturally made court, but it is free of maintenance and cleaning problems. The synthetic court is called the Mercury Grassphalts Court, and it is one of several new innovative types. Another court surface is usually called a *carpet*, and it is used for indoor tournaments on the professional tennis tour. The carpet is laid over whatever existing surface is available, and that combination produces a fast court that encourages a serve-volley game.

A final interesting point with tennis court surfaces is that hard and synthetic courts are smoothed or roughened depending on the amount of play and rally circumstances expected in a certain geographical area. A high altitude location will tend to have a roughened surface to provide more opportunity for baseline play, while courts in low altitudes will have a smoother surface, since the density of the air allows for more rally situations.

TENNIS RACKETS

Tennis rackets were at one time made of various woods, including ash or beech and combinations of perhaps sycamore, obeche, or mahogany. The wood racket was handcrafted, and the number of wood laminations indicated the quality of the racket. Some rackets are still made of wood in the 1980s, but they are often reinforced by graphite or fiberglass strips. Composite rackets are designed with a combination of nylon, polyurethane, carbon, fiber-glass, and graphite. Metal and aluminum rackets are still available, but as with wood rackets, they are being replaced by the composite racket.

Rackets have also changed in size over the last fifteen years ranging from a regular size, to a mid-size, to an oversize racket. The Prince racket was the first oversize racket, and now numerous companies are manufacturing similar ones. Shapes of racket heads range from pear-shaped to round and oblong.

Terms are used to describe the racket and what it is built to accomplish. A *stiff racket* is supposed to provide control, but minimize power. A *flexible racket* will give added power, but there will be less control of the shot. There are also combinations of stiffness and flexibility, with a graded identification of the extent of stiff play versus flexible play. Rackets are head light, balanced, and head heavy. They are light, semi-light, and medium in weight. The ideal area for contact with the ball is called a sweet spot, and it is located

Sweet Spot

below center, above center, elongated, and wide across center. Most sweet spots are located below center, but they do vary. Racket grips are measured from 4⅛ inches to 4⅞ inches, with the widely used grips ranging from 4¼ to 4⅝ inches. Grips are composed of several types of material, with leather being the most useful and popular.

Prices of rackets range from an inexpensive, and probably worthless, ten dollars to an exorbitant six hundred dollars. It is a small wonder that consumers are confused. The developing player should therefore use some kind of guide when purchasing a tennis racket.

The *guide to buying a racket* begins with price. It is acceptable to pay as much as one can afford, but the buyer should be reasonable. A good wood or metal racket can be bought for between twenty-five and sixty dollars. The best racket is what feels good, so the developing player should try several before selecting one to purchase. Most reputable tennis dealers will provide a loaner for practice for a charge of three to five dollars, then count that expense toward the purchase of a racket. Grip size should also be based to a great extent on how the grip feels, but a serve and volley

Assorted Tennis Rackets

player will want a larger grip than the baseline or all-purpose player. Most players buy a lightweight racket because it is easier to handle and places less stress on the elbow.

Rackets are purchased unstrung if they are of reasonable quality, and a decision has to be made regarding the type of string to use. There are two considerations to be made when *selecting string:* the type of string and the weight at which the racket should be strung. There are basically two types of string: an expensive gut string (twenty-five to forty dollars), primarily for highly skilled tournament players, and a nylon base string that wears for a longer time, is less expensive, and is hardly discernible from the gut string for the average player. Nylon string ranges from ten to thirty dollars, and the selection is almost endless. There are oil hole strings, solid core strings, and composite strings that are all forms of nylon. Most nylon strings are acceptable, and a middle price seems to be a logical choice. The weight at which the racket should be strung should follow the manufacturer's recommendation, and then as the player develops skill, the weight based on skill level and ability can be identified through a series of choices.

The developing tennis player must understand that the expenses associated with being a player and the purchase of a racket continue to the purchase of a second, or backup racket, and to a restringing of a racket every month or two during the tennis season(s). When the racket seems to have lost the zip it once had or

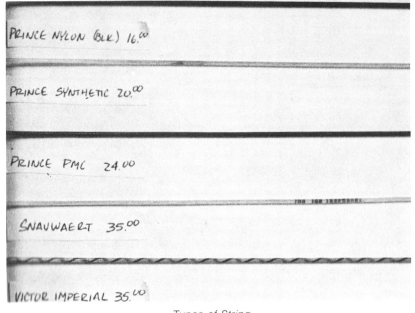

PRINCE NYLON (BLK) 16.00

PRINCE SYNTHETIC 20.00

PRINCE PMC 24.00

SNAUWAERT 35.00

VICTOR IMPERIAL 35.00

Types of String

the strings begin to fray, it is time to have the racket restrung. *Restringing* can consist of a full restring job or a technique called running repairs. If there is still life in the racket, and the player is not at a tournament level of play, a stringer can replace a brokenstring. A beginning player can have running repairs done on the racket and save a little.

Tennis Stringer

Tennis ball selection is another choice and expense to tennis play. A can of tennis balls ranges from two to four dollars and only lasts for two to three hours of play (if play is continuous and skillful). Discount stores and major sporting goods dealers often run specials for less than two dollars, but the player should be aware that there are many types of tennis balls for that price. For true bounce and longevity, balls should be

Tennis Balls

name-brand, and flaws or unknowns should be ignored. Pressurized balls don't last as long as hard core rubber tennis balls, but they are easier on elbows and they play with a true bounce. The hard core ball has a greater life expectancy but begins to bounce too high after extensive play. If a player lives at high altitude, the purchase of only high-altitude balls is worthwhile. There is a difference when playing at sea level and playing at 5,000 feet. Also, a two-ply, heavy-duty surface on the tennis ball will be worth the extra money in terms of longer wear.

TENNIS CLOTHING

The selection of *tennis shorts or skirt and a tennis top* is totally up to the player. An investment of ten dollars for a pair of shorts and a tee shirt to an investment of one hundred dollars for a designer pair of tennis shorts and top is the range for purchase of clothing. Tennis shoes and socks are a different matter expense-wise. The tennis shoe is designed for use on a tennis court and for the forward, backward, and lateral movement of the player. There are many stops and starts in tennis, and the toe of a tennis shoe is vulnerable to dragging and wearing out. Tennis shoes are sized as are dress shoes, and some tennis shoes also are measured by widths of wide or narrow. There are some subtle considerations when selecting a tennis shoe. It must have a firm insole and a good arch support. It is very important that the back portion of the shoe that rests against the Achilles' tendon be soft and pliable, and that there be an absorbent heel cushion.

A check to determine how much abuse the toe of the shoe will take will help the player avoid a new purchase every three or four weeks. If the tennis shoe fits the player, if it provides good support, and if it won't wear out in a few weeks, it will probably cost thirty-five dollars or more, but it is what the player ought to buy. Socks, although not expensive, should also be purchased with quality in mind. A tennis sock should absorb perspiration, fit well, and be designed for tennis play.

Tennis Shoes   *Tennis Socks*

Chapter Fifteen

Resources in Tennis

Part of developing as a tennis player is to participate in tournaments to develop skills in a pressure situation. Another growth area is continuing to learn the game by being aware of professional tennis organizations, and by staying up-to-date by reading tennis publications and other materials that will provide new ideas. These are the resources in tennis.

HOW TO GET STARTED IN TENNIS COMPETITION

The United States has a wide assortment of *tennis tournaments*. Those that are of most interest to the developing player are associated with recreation programs, college campus recreation programs, city tournaments, and club programs. There are tournaments for all types of players, from the novice beginner who is just now learning to hit a volley shot without ducking to a very skilled player. Tournaments usually are either ladder tournaments, single elimination or double elimination tournaments, inter-club, or a social round robin mixed doubles tournament. All are fun to play in with the correct perspective. Some are more competitive than others, and the player has to understand which are the more competitive and which are designed as a social function.

Ladder tournaments are found in all situations, including most campus recreation programs. They allow players to play at their own level by challenging individuals of similar skill, but positioned higher on the ladder based on earlier success demonstrated through winning. Club competition is a highly competitive league-type play in which records are kept and league standings are established. There are rewards for a team finishing first and second in a league, with a team or teams advancing to another round of competitive play. All programs have single and double elimination tournaments with ratings, including novice, C, B, A, and open divisions. Some are sanctioned by the United States Tennis Association (USTA) and require membership in that organization in order to participate.

Some tournaments are identified by a rating scale, usually through the USTA National Rating Tennis Program. There are also age division tournaments that have an open competition under 35 years of age, then an age division, including 35 and over, 40 and over, 45 and over, 55 and over, 65 and over, etc. Most single or double elimination tournaments are played through a period of a week and a player who wins may continue playing 5 or 6 matches if the play continues all the way to the championship. The number of matches depends on the size of a draw for the tournament (a draw is the number of entrants).

The *USTA National Rating Program* has become a popular device for rating players, not only for tournament play, but for social play to help people identify their level of skill so that a match can be an equal competition. The rating scale is established from 1.0 through 7.0. The lower the rating classification, the closer to a beginner, and the higher the rating, the closer to a professional player. The classification of 3.5 to 4.5 seems to be the typical club player rating and is probably a major first goal for a developing player. The beginner usually starts at the 1.0 through the 2.5 level and progresses rapidly through the early classifications. The rating program provides a descriptive version of each classification, and many tennis teachers are now able to use the rating objectively and systematically. Table 15.0 gives a view of the National Tennis Rating Program categories.

TENNIS INFORMATION

There are numerous textbooks and periodicals that help you to learn to play tennis and to continue to develop skills and knowledge associated with the game. There are also tennis associations designed to promote the game in community and tennis club environments.

The *United States Tennis Association* (USTA) is the most well-known agency or organization designed to promote tennis at every level of play and competition. To play in sanctioned USTA tournaments, membership in the USTA is required. The same group sponsors the National Tennis Rating Program. But, perhaps most important, the USTA supplies educational groups with an assortment of tennis publications and films. One publication circulated to members of the USTA is entitled *World Tennis*. This periodical also is sold at newsstands. Other publications by the USTA include general textbooks, material for group instruction and for teaching tennis,

Table 15.0
National Tennis Rating Program

SELF-RATING GUIDELINES

The National Tennis Rating Program provides a simple, initial self-placement method of grouping individuals of similar ability levels for league play, tournaments, group lessons, social competition and club or community programs.

The rating categories are generalizations about skill levels. You may find that you actually play above or below the category which best describes your skill level, depending on your competitive ability. The category you choose is not meant to be permanent, but may be adjusted as your skills change or as your match play demonstrates the need for reclassification.

To Place Yourself:

A. Begin with 1.0. Read all categories carefully and then decide which one best describes your present ability level.

B. Be certain that you qualify on all points of all preceding categories as well as those in the classification you choose.

C. When rating yourself assume you are playing against a player of the same sex and the same ability.

D. Your self-rating may be verified by a teaching professional, coach, league coordinator or other qualified expert.

E. The person in charge of your tennis program has the right to reclassify you if your self-placement is thought to be inappropriate.

NTRP RATING CATEGORIES

1.0	This player is just starting to play tennis.
1.5	This player has limited playing experience and is still working primarily on getting the ball over the net; has some knowledge of scoring but is not familiar with basic positions and procedures for singles and doubles play.
2.0	This player may have had some lessons but needs on-court experience; has obvious stroke weaknesses but is beginning to feel comfortable with singles and doubles play.
2.5	This player has more dependable strokes and is learning to judge where the ball is going; has weak court coverage or is often caught out of position, but is starting to keep the ball in play with other players of the same ability.
3.0	This player can place shots with moderate success; can sustain a rally of slow pace but is not comfortable with all strokes; lacks control when trying for power.
3.5	This player has achieved stroke dependability and direction on shots within reach, including forehand and backhand volleys, but still lacks depth and variety; seldom double faults and occasionally forces errors on the serve.
4.0	This player has dependable strokes on both forehand and backhand sides; has the ability to use a variety of shots including lobs, overheads, approach shots and volleys; can place the first serve and force some errors; is seldom out of position in a doubles game.

Table 15.0
National Tennis Rating Program (continued)

4.5	This player has begun to master the use of power and spins; has sound footwork; can control depth of shots and is able to move opponent up and back; can hit first serves with power and accuracy and place the second serve, is able to rush net with some success on serve in singles as well as doubles.
5.0	This player has good shot anticipation; frequently has an outstanding shot or exceptional consistency around which a game may be structured; can regularly hit winners or force errors off of short balls; can successfully execute lobs, drop shots, half volleys and overhead smashes; has good depth and spin on most second serves.
5.5	This player can execute all strokes offensively and defensively; can hit dependable shots under pressure; is able to analyze opponents' styles and can employ patterns of play to assure the greatest possibility of winning points; can hit winners or force errors with both first and second serves. Return of serve can be an offensive weapon.
6.0	This player has mastered all of the above skills; has developed power and/or consistency as a major weapon; can vary strategies and styles of play in a competitive situation. This player typically has had intensive training for national competition at junior or collegiate levels.
6.5	This player has mastered all of the above skills and is an experienced tournament competitor who regularly travels for competition and whose income may be partially derived from prize winnings.
7.0	This is a world class player.
PURPOSE	
1	The National Tennis Association has worked in close harmony with the United States Professional Tennis Association and the United States Tennis Association to make available to the tennis-playing public this simplified self-rating program.
2	The primary goal of the program is to help all tennis players enjoy the game by providing a method of classifying skill levels for more compatible matches, group lessons, league play, tournaments and other programs.
3	The National Tennis Rating Program is based on the premise that any placement program must be easy to administer, free, non-commercial and non-exclusive (in order to be universally accepted and effective).

strategy material, program planning, tennis information, and rules-regulations. A membership with the USTA is a small investment for the developing player, since membership is $8.00 for the junior player (under 21 years of age), and less than $20.00 for an adult. The benefits for a serious player are excellent, and the organization really does function for the promotion of tennis. The USTA membership address is: USTA/Box 1726/Hicksville, N.Y. 11802.

There are also tennis organizations affiliated with the USTA. These are described as *sectional offices and state organizations.* Both of these groups sponsor tennis tournaments and also have the major role of promoting tennis. With a USTA membership, the member also receives newsletters from sectional and state organizations. The local state and sectional organizations also rate players and carry on the work of the USTA at the local level.

Tennis publications, both trade and textbook, are extensive. Two additional magazines that may assist the developing player are *Tennis,* an instructional, informative magazine similar to *World Tennis,* and *Racquet Quarterly,* a surrealistic, esthetic publication that presents tennis as an art form. Three good tennis trade books include:

1. Vic Branden and Bill Bruns — *Tennis For The Future*
2. Paul Douglas — *The Handbook of Tennis*
3. W. Timothy Gallwey — *The Inner Tennis Game*

The textbook industry is also inundated with tennis books. Three that have been bestsellers in the past and that are used in college classes of tennis are:

1. Dick Gould — *Tennis Anyone?*
2. Clancy Moore and M. B. Chafin — *Tennis Everyone*
3. Chet Murphy — *Advanced Tennis*

One other good tennis resource for a player who continues to develop following group instruction at the college/university level is a *teaching professional.* As an occasional review, or to have technique analyzed, a teaching professional will be of value. There are several points to remember concerning a teaching professional, or for that matter, an instructor at the college level who teaches tennis. That professional should know mechanics of stroke execution, should know how to present the information in an interesting and informative way, and should be able to analyze stroke mistakes. Go to a teaching professional for lessons, then go back and play for an extended period. It doesn't make any difference what kind of stroke development occurs in lessons if that stroke can't be assimilated in tennis match conditions.

Resources are important for a developing tennis player. The selection of the proper resources is important, and must be done with some degree of insight. A player needs to keep up with changes in tennis, and needs to have enough knowledge to discuss tennis intelligently.

Chapter Sixteen

The Roots of Tennis

Tennis as a sport has existed for centuries, and its evolution has occurred in a somewhat dramatic fashion. The roots of tennis are deeply ingrained in sociological and historical perspective. Tennis has been adopted by society as a game that reflects certain societal values and concepts.

THE HISTORICAL PERSPECTIVE OF TENNIS IN THE UNITED STATES SINCE THE TURN OF THE CENTURY

Tennis, by 1900, was an international event with worldwide participation by the developing industrial nations. By the 1920s, the United States had emerged as a leading nation in tennis with numerous American players dominating the international scene. From 1920 through 1925, Bill Tilden, the early male great in tennis, remained undefeated. Early female players who dominated from 1920 to 1929 were Suzanne Langlen and Helen Wills Moody. In the 1930s, Don Budge and Alice Marble gained the attention of the international tennis world with Wimbledon victories, in 1938 by Budge and in 1939 by Marble. The first professional tennis tournament was played in 1926, and players including Langlen, Tilden, and Budge turned professional. Several strong American players developed in the 1940s and 1950s. In the 1950s Maureen Connolly and Althea Gibson, the first black international female tennis player of prestige, emerged as championship players, and Pancho Gonzales established himself as a leader in the men's division. In the 1960s, Billie Jean King, Chris Evert Lloyd, and Jimmy Connors became household names. Rules changed, and tie breakers became a part of a match, eliminating the long match with scores of 16-14, 5-7, 19-17. Professional tennis began to blossom with first men, then women, receiving the large purses. Wimbledon was the first major tournament to become an open, inviting both professionals and amateurs to compete in the same field. In 1960 there were over 5 million tennis players in the United States; by the late 1970s, there were in excess of 28 million. The increase in numbers slowed in the 1970s and early 1980s, but the popularity of the game continued with all age groups becoming active.

In the early years of tennis, role models in the amateur and professional tennis circuits provided the visibility for the game. Participation of the masses is at least partially attributed to those pioneers who dominated or competed so intensely for so many years. The game changed, the players became more skilled, and the average person began to play. Other reasons why tennis has become so popular relate to sociological factors.

THE SOCIOLOGICAL ASPECTS
OF TENNIS PARTICIPATION

Sociological perspectives of tennis are revealing as they reflect on tennis as a mirror of society. What happens in tennis is simply a microcosm of the larger society.

Tennis was an *acceptable activity for girls and women*. It was okay for the female to engage in a tennis match, since it was feminine-oriented. Women in the 1800s and at the turn of the century were expected to be ladylike and participate in so-called "feminine activities." A sport that encouraged that position was certainly acceptable to and generally approved by society. To demonstrate the evolution of that concept, it can be observed that the women's rights movement of the 1970s was followed by legislation that provided equal opportunities for all female athletes to participate in any sport effort. That legislation, of course, was the Educational Amendment Act of 1972 entitled Title IX.

Other events in history changed the game of tennis. The *advent of television* contributed in two ways. First, it brought the game and its role models into the homes of nearly all Americans. They were able to see how the game had changed, how the game was exciting, and how the skill aspect involved a superior form of physical effort. Second, television changed the face of the game. As a means of controlling the length of the game, television producers were able to effect a change from matches that lasted until a player won by two games to a tie breaker situation described in Chapter 9. Clothes and tennis balls changed colors to accommodate television production. The excitement, the means by which to end a match more abruptly, and the colorfulness of the game began to attract widespread interest in the game from the average person who was looking for a sports alternative.

Economics also played a major role in the growth of tennis. The professionalizing of the game, initially at Wimbledon and then extensively on the tennis tour, sent a message to the public that there was money in the game. When players began to earn six-figure yearly incomes, attitudes changed concerning who should play tennis. In early years the game was an aristocratic activity, played by the wealthy or those who were financially in the upper one-third. Access to tennis courts in tennis' early development was limited to country clubs and backyards of wealthy players. In the late 1960s, when tennis changed to a professional sport rather than mostly amateur, society experienced a change related to court facilities. Municipal courts were built to provide opportunities for individuals who were watching the change of the game on television and who were becoming increasingly aware that there was a possibility of earning money through tennis, either as a tennis professional or a teaching professional.

A final economic impact was the development of tennis clothing and equipment. The selling of these two commodities became a major business. When individuals began to play in large numbers, the business world jumped on the bandwagon. When participation swelled from 5 million in 1960 to more than 28 million by the late 1970s there had to be a provision for new, more brightly colored tennis clothes and an equipment industry that would provide quality tennis rackets. The public responded by purchasing millions of dollars worth of these products, providing an economic boost to the industry.

Female participants engaged in tennis from the early years to the more militant years characterized by the advent of Title IX. Television promoted tennis as an attractive sport event and changed the rules of the game. Money earned at professional tennis tournaments and on the tennis pro-circuit became an inducement for becoming a part of the tennis scene. Big business, through the manufacture and sale of tennis supplies, attempted to meet the demand for new tennis clothing and innovative equipment. Each of the changes in tennis and societal attitudes concerning tennis opened the door for the construction of public tennis courts, which opened the way for an influx of participants.

The Rating of Skill
by the Developing Player

The developing player is in need of being appraised skill wise if improvement is to continue. Two methods are available for the player through material in this guide. The developing player may use the USTA National Rating Tennis Program for identification of what level to play in tournaments and in friendly competition. The player may also use the following Skill Appraisal Chart to provide feedback regarding skill level.

The Skill Appraisal Chart breaks down the most important parts of the beginning and intermediate skills into a yes-no response, and provides a subjective rating for the player to judge skill. The yes-no response is a simple statement of "does the player execute that skill." If the skill can be executed, then a check by a yes is acceptable, and if the player does not execute the skill, then a check by the no is the only answer. It is difficult for the player to be subjective concerning personal skill, so it is suggested that the player should attempt to identify yes-no responses conservatively. There is also a rating scale devised to provide input of how well a player executes a skill if the response to the skill is yes. The rating is on a one to three basis, and is described as follows:

3. No changes necessary — the skill execution is specific to the mechanics of the stroke.
2. Average mechanics associated with the skill, with improvement a matter of practice and developing consistency.
1. Need some guidance in the development of the skill, and parts of the mechanics are not always correct.

Part of skill appraisal has to be the mental aspect of play, since without the mental, the physical aspect will decline and progress to identified limits. The rating of the mental area of tennis is the same scale of one to three as for the skill appraisal:

3. Excellent mental consistency; seldom a breakdown.
2. Developing steadily in this area, and there is more success than failure involved in the mental.
1. Difficulty with the mental part; the concept doesn't seem to be consistent at this point.

Again, there is only a rating if the first response is yes to the yes-no section.

There are 75 possible selections to be made on the skill appraisal checklist, with 225 possible points that can be accumulated. A score of:

175-225 points = outstanding progress.
125-174 points = good sound progress.
 75-124 points = a lot of room for improvement, but the development is occurring.
  0-74 points = a major concern that progress is minimal.

Of the 10 choices in the mental area, an accumulation of 30 points can occur. A 20-30 point measure indicates that the mental aspect of the game is strong. Point accumulation of 10-19 indicates that there is marked development in the mental game. The scores of 0-9 are a cause for concern that the mental may be interfering with the mechanics of play.

SKILL APPRAISAL

SKILL DESCRIPTION	SKILL EXECUTION		
	YES	NO	RATING
Groundstroke Ready Position:			
1. Legs bent.			
2. Sitting position.			
3. Racket up above hands.			
4. Feet parallel and shoulder width apart.			
5. Weight on the balls of the feet.			
Groundstroke Forehand:			
1. Turns shoulder early.			
2. Brings racket back in early preparation.			
3. Feet pivot in timing with shoulder and racket.			
4. Transfer of weight into the ball from backswing to contact (steps into the ball).			
5. Follow through is firm and high.			
Groundstroke Backhand:			
1. Turns shoulder early.			
2. Brings racket back in early preparation.			
3. Feet pivot in timing with shoulder and racket.			
4. Changes grip as the racket is brought into backswing position.			
5. Transfer of weight into the ball from backswing to contact (steps into the ball).			
6. Follow through is firm and high.			
Topspin Groundstroke Changes:			
1. Grip change for forehand to western grip.			
2. Brings racket back low during preparation.			
3. Extreme bend of legs on preparation.			
4. Racket path low to high on the follow through.			

SKILL APPRAISAL

SKILL DESCRIPTION	SKILL EXECUTION		
	YES	NO	RATING
Topspin Groundstroke Changes:			
5. Transfers weight and steps into the ball, extending legs up.			
6. Rolls wrist at contact through follow through.			
Slice Groundstroke Changes:			
1. Brings racket back in a high preparation.			
2. Racket path high to low to slightly high.			
3. Hits the ball with an open racket face.			
4. Follows through with an open racket face.			
Volley:			
1. Uses continental grip and then "cheats" to a forehand or backhand eastern grip.			
2. Blocks or punches the ball out in front.			
3. Short backswing.			
4. Short follow through with the edge of bottom of racket leading slightly.			
5. Cross-steps to hit all balls except those directly at the body.			
6. Stays low on the ball.			
Service:			
1. Toss is a lifting and placement motion with arm straight.			
2. Feet are parallel and shoulder width apart.			
3. Racket is brought back to the middle of the shoulder blades on preparation.			
4. Grip is a continental grip.			
5. Toss is off the lead shoulder higher than the racket reach.			
6. Contact with the ball is a flat racket face with the wrist breaking over and through the ball.			
7. Follow through is off the opposite leg and low.			
Topspin Service Changes:			
1. Toss is above the head.			

SKILL APPRAISAL

SKILL DESCRIPTION	SKILL EXECUTION		
	YES	NO	RATING
Topspin Service Changes:			
2. Contact with the ball is a brushing up and over the ball with a slight angle to the ball.			
3. The body is coiled with a pronounced leg bend at backswing position.			
4. Back foot is parallel to, but behind the lead foot.			
Slice Service Changes:			
1. Toss is in the middle of the body and lower than the other two serves.			
2. Contact with the ball is on the back-side of slightly under center.			
3. Back foot is parallel to, but behind, the lead foot (half way between basic flat and topspin).			
4. Body is open at contact.			
Return of Service:			
1. Player is relaxed in ready position.			
2. Early turn of shoulder.			
3. Shortened backswing.			
4. Block of all fast-paced serves.			
5. Short follow through of service.			
Overhead Smashes:			
1. Settles underneath the ball.			
2. Racket rests between shoulder blades with elbow "up" at right angle.			
3. Feet are spread shoulder width apart and parallel.			
4. Coils the body under the ball.			
5. Follow through is to opposite leg and down, but shorter than a serve.			
6. Scissors kick is an exchange of foot position while in midair.			
7. Contact of ball is square with a break of the wrist.			
Lobs:			
1. Player must bend and then extend legs.			

SKILL APPRAISAL

SKILL DESCRIPTION	SKILL EXECUTION		
	YES	NO	RATING
Lobs:			
2. Lifting action.			
3. **Defensive lob** is high with the follow through slightly across the body.			
4. **Defensive underspin lob** is hit high with the follow through remaining in the same plane.			
5. **Topspin lob** is hit with a trajectory just over the outstretched arm of opponent, and the follow through is across the body with a roll of the wrist.			
6. **Moonball** is hit with soft pace and extra wrist roll with low trajectory compared with topspin lob.			
7. **Above racket blocks** have no backswing or follow through, just a punch.			
Other Shots Used:			
1. **Approach Shots** — short backswing, short follow through, keeps ball in the court.			
2. **Half Volleys** — short backswing, short follow through, stays low on the ball throughout the swing.			
3. **Two-hand Backhands** — keeps arms close to the body; adjusts backswing for flat, slice, and topspin strokes. Grip is snug, with dominant hand the bottom hand on the backhand and the top hand on the forehand.			

MENTAL DESCRIPTION	SKILL EXECUTION		
	YES	NO	RATING
1. Concentration on the ball seams.			
2. Can read the body language of the opponent.			
3. Relaxed position prior to beginning of play.			
4. Relaxed attitude when executing strokes.			
5. Thinking about strategy ahead of the play.			
6. Controlling temper and angry outbursts.			
7. Self talk is positive.			
8. Elimination of fear of failure.			
9. Elimination of fear of winning.			
10. Elimination of opponent's effort to "psyche out" the player.			

Glossary of
Tennis Terms

Ad: In a tie game, ad represents advantage of one point ot the server or receiver.

Ad court: The left service court.

Ad in: Advantage to the server.

Ad out: Advantage to the receiver.

American twist service: Serve that has a reverse side spin applied to the ball.

Anxiety: State of mental pressure that causes a reduction in physical performance.

Approach shot: A groundstroke hit inside the baseline toward the net.

Australian doubles: A two-player alignment in doubles that places both players in line perpendicular to the net.

Backhand: Balls hit on the non-racket side of the body.

Ballistic warm-up: Physically moving the body to prepare for a match.

Baseline: The end of the court located 39 feet from the net.

Center mark: The division line on the baseline that separates the right side from the left side.

Center strap: The strap that anchors the middle of the net to the court at a 3-foot height.

Chop: An exaggerated slice stroke.

Closed face: Position of the racket face as it is turned down toward the court.

Conventional doubles: Two players in a doubles match who move in a tandem.

Close in: Move in on the net following an approach shot, an overhead smash, or a volley.

Cross Court: Hitting the ball at an angle across the width of the court with the net as the central boundary.

Defensive lob: A ball hit to give the defending player a chance to recover from an offensive shot.

Deuce: A tie score in games at 40-40 or beyond.

Dink shot: A side spin drop shot hit at an angle from the net to the other side of the court.

Division of play: The division of the court between the opponent's position and the other player's position that provides an equal distance to reach a forehand or backhand shot.

Double fault: The serving of two illegal serves during one service point.

Down the line: A shot hit down a sideline in a direct line from the player.

Drive: A ball hit with force.

Drop shot: A ball hit from a groundstroke position that barely clears the net and dies on the opponent's side of the court.

Drop volley: Same shot as drop shot, but from a position of hitting the ball before it bounces on the court.

Dump shot: A push action that guides the ball to an open area beyond the opponent's side of the court.

Etiquette: Rules of behavior on a tennis court.

Fault: An illegally hit serve.

Flat serve: A serve hit with little spin and with a basically flat trajectory.

Flexible racket: A description of a racket that has a great amount of power and less control.

Forecourt: Part of the tennis court between the net and the service court line.

Forehand: Balls hit on the racket side of the body.

Groundstroke: The act of hitting a ball following the bounce of the ball on the court.

Half volley: A ball hit immediately following the bounce on the court.

Homebase: A term to describe the player who prefers to play from the baseline and rally.

Let: A point played over due to interference or a serve replayed due to an otherwise legal serve touching the net.

Lob: A ball hit up over the net player, driving that player back away from the net.

Love: A zero score.

Match: The best of two of three sets in most play situations.

Moonball: A lofted topspin shot that is designed to change the pace of a rally. Halfway between a lob and a groundstroke.

Net play: Generally, offensive play near the net with volley shots and overheads characteristic of the shots hit.

No-man's land: The area between the baseline and the service court line that a player should never set up in to rally.

Non-racket shoulder: A term to describe the position of players in relation to the ball or court. The side of the body on which the racket is not grasped (e.g., right-hand player's non-racket shoulder is the left shoulder).

Non-racket side of the body: The same description as for non-racket shoulder, but refers to the whole side of the body (e.g., right-handed player's left side of the body).

Offensive lob: A lofted shot hit deep to the opponent's baseline with topspin ball action.

Open face: Position of the racket face as it is turned up to the sky.

Orthodox overhead smash: An overhead smash that requires no foot position exchange.

Overhead jump smash: Includes a scissors kick in addition to the orthodox overhead smash as the player jumps to hit the ball.

Overhead smash: An offensive throwing action stroke similar to a serve in motion, but delivered at the net back to the baseline.

Pace: A ball hit with the same consistency, usually with some degree of velocity.

Percentage tennis: A philosophical strategy that is based on the opponent making the error rather than hitting all winning shots.

Punching action: Hitting the ball with little backswing or follow through.

Racket face: The strings of the racket as they face the oncoming ball during a stroke sequence.

Racket head: The total racket area that includes the string and the material around the face.

Racket shoulder: The shoulder of the arm with which the player grasps the racket.

Racket side of the body: Same description as for the racket shoulder but includes the whole side of the body.

Rally: A sustained play of a point, usually associated with hitting only groundstrokes from the baseline area. It never refers to hitting a ball on the fly as in a volley.

Return of serve: The act of hitting a ball back off a serve.

Service court line: The line that is the base of the service courts and that is parallel to the net and baseline.

Set: Represents the winning of six games by a margin of 2 games, or winning by a score of 7-5 or 7-6.

Sidespin: Spin action imparted on a ball so that the ball will land on the court and kick away from the person hitting the ball. Ball is hit on the backside portion to give the side spin effect.

Slice serve: A serve hit with side spin.

Social doubles: Tennis played in a friendly atmosphere with a player alignment of one up-one back.

Stiff racket: A description of a racket that has good control and less power.

Strategy: The planning of an attack when competing against another player or a doubles team.

Stretch warm-up: A static stretching of muscle groups to prepare for a match.

Swinging action: A groundstroke movement that represents the motor pattern of swinging as in a baseball bat swing.

Throwing action: A serving or overhead smash motion that represents a throwing pattern as in throwing a baseball.

Timing: The final coordinated effort to hit a ball at the right synchronized point.

Topspin: A ball hit with an overspin rotation action.

Topspin serve: A serve that has a forward or overspin rotation applied to the ball. The end result is a high-bouncing, quick rebound from the tennis court.

Underspin: A ball hit with backspin rotation. The ball will have a tendency to float and slow down when striking the tennis court.

Warming up: The act of physically preparing for a tennis match.

Warming down: The act of cooling off the body in a sequential logical order to complete the finish of a tennis match.

USTA Rules of Tennis and Cases and Decisions, 1983

RULES OF TENNIS

Explanatory Note

The following Rules and Cases and Decisions are the official Code of the International Tennis Federation, of which the United States Tennis Association is a member. USTA Comments and USTA Cases and Decisions have the same weight and force in USTA tournaments as do ITF Cases and Decisions.

When a match is played without officials the principles and guidelines set forth in the USTA Publication, The Code, shall apply in any situation not covered by the rules.

The caption above each rule was inserted by the USTA Rules Committee, not by the ITF, to indicate the content of the rule but not in any way to limit its scope.

A vertical line in the margin by a rule indicates a change or amendment made by the ITF in September, 1982, and which took effect January, 1983.

THE SINGLES GAME

RULE 1

Dimensions and Equipment

The court shall be a rectangle 78 feet (23.77m.) long and 27 feet (8.23m.) wide. **USTA Comment:** *See Rule 35 for a doubles court.*

It shall be divided across the middle by a net suspended from a cord or metal cable of a maximum diameter of one-third of an inch (0.8cm.), the ends of which shall be attached to, or pass over, the tops of two posts, which shall be not more than 6 inches (15cm.) in diameter. The centres of the posts shall be 3 feet (0.91m.) outside the court on each side and the height of the posts shall be such that the top of the cord or metal cable shall be 3 feet 6 inches (1.07m.) above the ground.

When a combined doubles (see Rule 35) and singles court with a doubles net is used for singles, the net must be supported to a height of 3 feet 6 inches (1.07m.) by means of two posts, called "singles sticks", which shall be not more than 3 inches (7.5cm.) square or 3 inches (7.5cm.) in diameter. The centres of the singles sticks shall be 3 feet (0.91m.) outside the singles court on each side.

The net shall be extended fully so that it fills completely the space between the two posts and shall be of sufficiently small mesh to prevent the ball passing through. The height of the net shall be 3 feet (0.914m.) at the centre, where it shall be held down taut by a strap not more than 2 inches (5cm.) wide and completely white in colour. There shall be a band covering the cord or metal cable and the top of the net of not less than 2 inches (5cm.) nor more than two and a half inches (6.3cm.) in depth on each side and completely white in colour.

There shall be no advertisement on the net, strap, band or singles sticks.

The lines bounding the ends and sides of the Court shall respectively be called the base-lines and the side-lines. On each side of the net, at a distance of 21 feet (6.40m.) from it and parallel with it, shall be drawn the service-lines. The space on each side of the net between the service-line and the side-lines shall be divided into two equal parts called the service-courts by the centre service-line, which must be 2 inches (5cm.) in width, drawn half-way between, and parallel with, the side-lines. Each base-line shall be bisected by an imaginary continuation of the centre service-line to a line 4

'Reprinted by permission of the United States Tennis Association.

inches (10cm.) in length and 2 inches (5cm.) in width called the centre mark drawn inside the Court, at right angles to and in contact with such base-lines. All other lines shall be not less than 1 inch (2.5cm.) nor more than 2 inches (5cm.) in width, except the base-line, which may be 4 inches (10cm.) in width, and all measurements shall be made to the outside of the lines.

If advertising or any other material is placed at the back of the court, it may not contain white or yellow, or any other light colour.

If advertisements are placed on the chairs of the Linesmen sitting at the back of the court, they may not contain white or yellow.

Note: In the case of the International Tennis Championship (Davis Cup) or other Official Championships of the International Federation, there shall be a space behind each baseline of not less than 21 feet (6.4m.), and at the sides of not less than 12 feet (3.66m.).

USTA Comment: *It is important to have a stick 3 feet, 6 inches long, with a notch cut in at the 3-foot mark for the purpose of measuring the height of the net at the posts and in the center. These measurements always should be made before starting to play a match.*

RULE 2

Permanent Fixtures

The permanent fixtures of the Court shall include not only the net, posts, singles sticks, cord or metal cable, strap and band, but also, where there are any such, the back and side stops, the stands, fixed or movable seats and chairs round the Court, and their occupants, all other fixtures around and above the Court, and the Umpire, Net-cord Judge, Foot-fault Judge, Linesmen and Ball Boys when in their respective places.

Note: For the purpose of this Rule, the word "Umpire" comprehends the Umpire, the persons entitled to a seat on the Court, and all those persons designated to assist the Umpire in the conduct of a match.

RULE 3

Ball — Size, Weight and Bound

The ball shall have a uniform outer surface and shall be white or yellow in colour. If there are any seams, they shall be stitchless.

The ball shall be more than two and a half inches (6.35cm.) and less than two and five-eighths inches (6.67cm.) in diameter, and more than two ounces (56.7 grams) and less than two and one-sixteenth ounces (58.5 grams) in weight.

The ball shall have a bound of more than 53 inches (135cm.) and less than 58 inches (147cm.) when dropped 100 inches (254cm.) upon a concrete base.

The ball shall have a forward deformation of more than .220 of an inch (.56 cm.) and less than .290 of an inch (.74cm.) and a return deformation of more than .350 of an inch (.89cm.) and less than .425 of an inch (1.08cm.) at 18 lb. (8.165kg.) load. The two deformation figures shall be the averages of three individual readings along three axes of the ball and no two individual readings shall differ by more than .030 of an inch (.08cm.) in each case.

All tests for bound, size and deformation shall be made in accordance with the Regulations in the Appendix hereto.

RULE 4

The Racket

Rackets failing to comply with the following specifications are not approved for play under the Rules of Tennis:

(a) The hitting surface of the racket shall be flat and consist of a pattern of crossed strings connected to a frame and alternately interlaced or bonded where they cross; and the stringing pattern shall be generally uniform, and in particular not less dense in the centre than in any other area.

(b) The frame of the racket shall not exceed 32 inches (81.28cm.) in overall length, including the handle and 12½ inches (31.75cm.) in overall width. The strung surface shall not exceed 15½ inches (39.37cm.) in overall length, and 11½ inches (29.21cm.) in overall width.

(c) The frame, including the handle, and the strings:

(i) shall be free of attached objects and protrusions, other than those utilized solely and specifically to limit or prevent wear and tear or vibration, or to distribute weight, and which are reasonable in size and placement for such purposes; and

(ii) shall be free of any device which makes it possible for a player to change materially the shape of the racket.

The International Tennis Federation shall rule on the question of whether any racket or prototype complies with the above specifications or is otherwise approved, or not approved, for play. Such ruling may be undertaken on its own initiative, or upon application by any party with a bona fide interest therein, including any player, equipment manufacturer or National Association or members thereof. Such rulings and applications shall be made in accordance with the applicable Review and Hearing Procedures of the International Tennis Federation, copies of which may be obtained from the office of the Secretary.

RULE 5

Server and Receiver

The players shall stand on opposite sides of the net; the player who first delivers the ball shall be called the Server, and the other the Receiver.

Case 1. Does a player, attempting a stroke, lose the point if he crosses an imaginary line in the extension of the net?

(a) before striking the ball?

(b) after striking the ball?

Decision. He does not lose the point in either case by crossing the imaginary line and provided he does not enter the lines bounding his opponent's Court (Rule 20 (e). In regard to hindrance, his opponent may ask for the decision of the Umpire under Rules 21 and 25.

Case 2. The Server claims that the Receiver must stand within the lines bounding his Court. Is this necessary?

Decision. No. The Receiver may stand wherever he pleases on his own side of the net.

RULE 6

Choice of Ends and Service

The choice of ends and the right to be Server or Receiver in the first game shall be decided by toss. The player winning the toss may choose or require his opponent to choose:

(a) The right to be Server or Receiver, in which case the other player shall choose the end; or

(b) The end, in which case the other player shall choose the right to be Server or Receiver.

USTA Comment: *These choices should be made promptly and are irrevocable.*

RULE 7

Delivery of Service

The service shall be delivered in the following manner. Immediately before commencing to serve, the Server shall stand with both feet at rest behind (i.e., further from the net than) the base-line, and within the imaginary continuations of the centre-mark and side-line. The Server shall then project the ball by hand into the air in any direction and before it hits the ground strike it with his racket, and the delivery shall be deemed to have been completed at the moment of the impact of the racket and the ball. A player with the use of only one arm may utilize his racket for the projection.

USTA Comment: *The service begins when the Server takes a ready position and ends when his racket makes contact with the ball, or when he misses the ball in attempting to serve it.*

Case 1. May the Server in a singles game take his stand behind the portion of the base-line between the side-lines of the Singles Court and the Doubles Court?

Decision. No.

Case 2. If a player, when serving, throws up two or more balls instead of one, does he lose that service?

Decision. No. A let should be called, but if the Umpire regards the action as deliberate he may take action under Rule 21.

USTA Case 3. May a player serve underhand?

Decision. Yes. There is no restriction regarding the kind of service which may be used; that is, the player may use an underhand or overhand service at his discretion.

RULE 8

Foot Fault

The Server shall throughout the delivery of the service:

(a) Not change his position by walking or running.

(b) Not touch, with either foot, any area other than that behind the base-line within the imaginary extension of the centre mark and side-line.

Note: The following interpretation of Rule 8 was approved by the International Tennis Federation on 9th July, 1958:

(a) The Server shall not, by slight movements of the feet which do not materially affect the location originally taken up by him, be deemed "to change his position by walking or running".

(b) The word "foot" means the extremity of the leg below the ankle.

USTA Comment: *This rule covers the most decisive stroke in the game, and there is no justification for its not being obeyed by players and enforced by officials. No official has the right to instruct any umpire to disregard violations of it. It is the prerogative of the Receiver, or his partner, or call foot faults, but only after all efforts (appeal to the server, requests for an umpire, etc.) have failed, and the foot faulting is so flagrant as to be clearly perceptible from the Receiver's side.*

RULE 9

From Alternate Courts

(a) In delivering the service, the Server shall stand alternately behind the right and left Courts beginning from the right in every game. If service from a wrong half of the Court occurs and is undetected, all play resulting from such wrong service or services shall stand, but the inaccuracy of station shall be corrected immediately it is discovered.

(b) The ball served shall pass over the net and hit the ground within the Service Court which is diagonally opposite, or upon any line bounding such Court, before the Receiver returns it.

RULE 10

Faults

The Service is a fault:

(a) If the Server commit any breach of Rules 7, 8 or 9;

(b) If he miss the ball in attempting to strike it;

(c) If the ball served touch a permanent fixture (other than the net, strap or band) before it hits the ground.

Case 1. After throwing a ball up preparatory to serving, the Server decides not to strike at it and catches it instead. Is it a fault?

Decision. No.

Case 2. In serving in a singles game played on a Doubles Court with doubles posts and singles sticks, the ball hits a singles stick and then hits the ground within the lines of the correct Service Court. Is this a fault or a let?

Decision. In serving it is a fault, because the singles stick, the doubles post, and that portion of the net, or band between them are permanent fixtures. (Rules 2 and 10, and note to Rule 24.)

USTA Comment: *The significant point governing Case 2 is that the part of the net and band "outside" the singles sticks is not part of the net over which this singles match is being played. Thus such a serve is a fault under the provisions of Article (c) above . . . By the same token, this would be a fault also if it were a singles game played with permanent posts in the singles position. (See Case 1 under Rule 24 for difference between "service" and "good return" with respect to a ball's hitting a net post.)*

USTA Comment: *In matches played without umpires it is customary for the Receiver to determine whether the service is good or a fault. Indeed, each player makes the calls for all balls to hit his side of the net. In doubles, the Receiver's partner makes the calls with respect to the service line.*

RULE 11

Service After a Fault

After a fault (if it be the first fault) the Server shall serve again from behind the same half of the Court from which he served that fault, unless the service was from the wrong half, when, in accordance with Rule 9, the Server shall be entitled to one service only from behind the other half.

Case 1. A player serves from a wrong Court. He loses the point and then claims it was a fault because of his wrong station.

Decision. This point stands as played and the next service should be from the correct station according to the score.

Case 2. The point score being 15 all, the Server, by mistake, serves from the left-hand Court. He wins the point. He then serves again from the right-hand Court, delivering a fault. This mistake in station is then discovered. Is he entitled to the previous point? From which Court should he next serve?

Decision. The previous point stands. The next service should be from the left-hand Court, the score being 30/15, and the Server has served one fault.

RULE 12

Receiver Must Be Ready

The Server shall not serve until the Receiver is ready. If the latter attempt to return the service, he shall be deemed ready. If, however, the Receiver signify that he is not ready, he may not claim a fault because the ball does not hit the ground within the limits fixed for the service.

USTA Comment: *The Server must wait until the Receiver is ready for the second service as well as the first, and if the Receiver claims to be not ready and does not make any effort to return a service, the Server may not claim the point, even though the service was good.*

RULE 13

A Let

In all cases where a let has to be called under the rules, or to provide for an interruption to play, it shall have the following interpretations:

(a) When called solely in respect of a service that one service only shall be replayed.

(b) When called under any other circumstance, the point shall be replayed.

USTA Comment: *A service that touches the net in passing yet falls into the proper court (or touches the receiver) is a let. This word is used also when, because of an interruption while the ball is in play, or for any other reason, a point is to be replayed. A spectator's outcry (of "out", "fault" or other) is not a valid basis for replay of a point, but action should be taken to prevent a recurrence.*

Case 1. A service is interrupted by some cause outside those defined in Rule 14. Should the service only be replayed?

Decision. No, the whole point must be replayed.

USTA Comment: *The phrase "in respect of a service" in (a) means a let because a served ball has touched the net before landing in the proper court, OR because the Receiver was not ready . . . Case 1 refers to a second* serve, and the decision means that if the interruption occurs during delivery of the second service, the Server gets two serves. *Example: On a second service a linesman calls "fault" and immediately corrects it (the Receiver meanwhile having let the ball go by). The Server is entitled to two serves, on this ground: The corrected call means that the Server has put the ball into play with a good service, and once the ball is in play and a let is called, the point must be replayed . . . Note, however, that if the serve were an unmistakable ace —that is, the Umpire was sure the erroneous call had no part in the Receiver's inability to play the ball — the point should be declared for the Server.*

Case 2. If a ball in play becomes broken, should a let be called?

Decision. Yes.

USTA Comment: *A ball shall be regarded as having become "broken" if, in the opinion of the Chair Umpire, it is found to have lost compression to the point of being unfit for further play, or unfit for any reason, and it is clear the defective ball was the one in play.*

RULE 14

The Service Is A Let

The service is a let:

(a) If the ball served touch the net, strap or band, and is otherwise good, or, after touching the net, strap or band, touch the Receiver or anything which he wears or carries before hitting the ground.

(b) If a service or a fault be delivered when the Receiver is not ready (see Rule 12).

In case of a let, that particular service shall not count, and the Server shall serve again, but a service let does not annul a previous fault.

RULE 15

When Receiver Becomes Server

At the end of the first game the Receiver shall become Server, and the Server Receiver; and so on alternately in all the subsequent games of a match. If a player serve out of turn, the player who ought to have served shall serve as soon as the mistake is discovered, but all points scored before such discovery shall be reckoned. If a game shall have been completed before such discovery, the order of service remains as altered. A fault served before such discovery shall not be reckoned.

RULE 16

When Players Change Ends

The player shall change ends at the end of the first, third and every subsequent alternate game of each set, and at the end of each set unless the total number of games in such set be even, in which case the change is not made until the end of the first game of the next set.

If a mistake is made and the correct sequence is not followed the players must take up their correct station as soon as the discovery is made and follow their original sequence.

RULE 17

Ball in Play Till Point Decided

A ball is in play from the moment at which it is delivered in service. Unless a fault or a let be called it remains in play until the point is decided.

USTA Comment: *A point is not "decided" simply when, or because, a good shot has clearly passed a player, or when an apparently bad shot passes over a baseline or sideline. An outgoing ball is still definitely "in play" until it actually strikes the ground, backstop or a permanent fixture, or a player. The same applies to a good ball, bounding after it has landed in the proper court. A ball that becomes imbedded in the net is out of play.*

Case 1. A player fails to make a good return. No call is made and the ball remains in play. May his opponent later claim the point after the rally has ended?

Decision. No. The point may not be claimed if the players continue to play after the error has been made, provided the opponent was not hindered.

USTA Comment: *To be valid, an out call on A's shot to B's court must be made before B's return has either gone out of play or has been hit by A. See Case 1 under Rule 30.*

USTA Case 2. A ball is played into the net; the player on the other side, thinking that the ball is coming over, strikes at it and hits the net. Who loses the point?

Decision. If the player touched the net while the ball was still in play, he loses the point.

RULE 18

Server Wins Point

The Server wins the point:

(a) If the ball served, not being a let under Rule 14, touch the Receiver or anything which he wears or carries, before it hits the ground;

(b) If the Receiver otherwise loses the point as provided by Rule 20.

RULE 19

Receiver Wins Point

The Receiver wins the point:

(a) If the Server serve two consecutive faults;

(b) If the Server otherwise lose the point as provided by Rule 20.

RULE 20

Player Loses Point

A player loses the point if:

(a) He fail, before the ball in play has hit the ground twice consecutively, to return it directly over the net (except as provided in Rule 24(a) or (c)); or

(b) He return the ball in play so that it hits the ground, a permanent fixture, or other object, outside any of the lines which bound his opponent's Court (except as provided in Rule 24(a) or (c)); or

USTA Comment: *A ball hitting a scoring device or other object attached to a net post results in loss of point to the striker.*

(c) He volley the ball and fail to make a good return even when standing outside the Court; or

(d) In playing the ball he deliberately carries or catches it on his racket or deliberately touches it with his racket more than once; or

USTA Comment: *Only when there is a definite "second push" by the player does his shot become illegal, with consequent loss of point. It should be noted that the word "deliberately" is the key word in this Rule and that two hits occurring in the course of a single continuous stroke would not be deemed a double hit.*

(e) He or his racket (in his hand or otherwise) or anything which he wears or carries touch the net, posts, singles sticks, cord or metal cable, strap or band, or the ground within his opponent's Court at any time while the ball is in play; or

USTA Comment: *Touching a pipe support that runs across the court at the bottom of the net is interpreted as touching the net; See USTA Comment under Rule 23.*

(f) He volley the ball before it has passed the net; or

(g) The ball in play touch him or anything that he wears or carries, except his racket in his hand or hands; or

USTA Comment: *This loss of point occurs regardless of whether the player is inside or outside the bounds of his court when the ball touches him. Except for a ball used in a first service fault, a player is considered to be "wearing or carrying" anything that he was wearing or carrying at the beginning of the*

point during which the touch occurred. Exception: *If an object worn or carried by a player falls to the ground and a ball hit by his opponent hits that object, then (1) if the ball falls outside the court, the opponent loses the point; (2) if the ball falls inside the court, a let is to be called.*

(h) He throws his racket at and hits the ball; or

(i) He deliberately and materially changes the shape of his racket during the playing of the point.

Case 1. In delivering a first service which falls outside the proper Court, the Server's racket slips out of his hand and flies into the net. Does he lose the point?

Decision. If his racket touches the net whilst the ball is in play, the Server loses the point (Rule 20 *(e)*).

Case 2. In serving, the racket flies from the Server's hand and touches the net before the ball has touched the ground. Is this a fault, or does the player lose the point?

Decision. The Server loses the point because his racket touches the net whilst the ball is in play (Rule 20 *(e)*).

Case 3. A and B are playing against C and D. A is serving to D. C touches the net before the ball touches the ground. A fault is then called because the service falls outside the Service Court. Do C and D lose the point?

Decision. The call "fault" is an erroneous one. C and D had already lost the point before "fault" could be called, because C touched the net whilst the ball was in play (Rule 20 *(e)*).

Case 4. May a player jump over the net into his opponent's Court while the ball is in play and not suffer penalty?

Decision. No. He loses the point (Rule 20 *(e)*).

Case 5. A cuts the ball just over the net, and it returns to A's side. B, unable to reach the ball, throws his racket and hits the ball. Both racket and ball fall over the net on A's Court. A returns the ball outside of B's Court. Does B win or lose the point?

Decision. B loses the point (Rule 20 *(e)* and *(h)*).

Case 6. A player standing outside the service Court is struck by a service ball before it has touched the ground. Does he win or lose the point?

Decision. The player struck loses the point (Rule 20 *(g)*), except as provided under Rule 14 *(a)*.

Case 7. A player standing outside the Court volleys the ball or catches it in his hand and claims the point because the ball was certainly going out of court.

Decision. In no circumstances can he claim the point:

(1) If he catches the ball he loses the point under Rule 20 *(g)*.

(2) If he volleys it and makes a bad return he loses the point under Rule 20 *(c)*.

(3) If he volleys it and makes a good return, the rally continues.

RULE 21

Player Hinders Opponent

If a player commits any act which hinders his opponent in making a stroke, then, if this is deliberate, he shall lose the point or if involuntary, the point shall be replayed.

Case 1. Is a player liable to a penalty if in making a stroke he touches his opponent?

Decision. No, unless the Umpire deems it necessary to take action under Rule 21.

Case 2. When a ball bounds back over the net, the player concerned may reach over the net in order to play the ball. What is the ruling if the player is hindered from doing this by his opponent?

Decision. In accordance with Rule 21, the Umpire may either award the point to the player hindered, or order the point to be replayed. (See also Rule 25.)

Case 3. Does an involuntary double hit constitute an act which hinders an opponent within Rule 21?

Decision. No.

USTA Comment: *Upon appeal by a competitor that an opponent's action in discarding a "second ball" after a rally has started constitutes a distraction (hindrance), the Umpire, if he deems the claim valid, shall require the opponent to make some other and satisfactory disposition of the ball. Failure to comply with this instruction may result in loss of point(s) or disqualification.*

USTA Comment: *'Deliberate' means a player did what he intended to do, although the resulting effect on his opponent might or might not have been what he intended. Example: a player, after his return is in the air, gives advice to his partner in such a loud voice that his opponent is hindered. 'Involuntary' means a non-intentional act such as a hat blowing off or a scream resulting from a sudden wasp sting.*

RULE 22

Ball Falling on Line — Good

A ball falling on a line is regarded as falling in the Court bounded by that line.

USTA Comment: *In matches played without officials, it is customary for each player to make the calls on all balls hit to his side of the net, and if a player cannot call a ball out with surety he should regard it as good. See The Code.*

RULE 23

Ball Touching Permanent Fixture

If the ball in play touch a permanent fixture (other than the net, posts, singles sticks, cord or metal cable, strap or band) after it has hit the ground, the player who struck it wins the point; if before it hits the ground, his opponent wins the point.

Case 1. A return hits the Umpire or his chair or stand. The player claims that the ball was going into Court.

Decision. He loses the point.

USTA Comment: *A ball in play that after passing the net strikes a pipe support running across the court at the base of the net is* regarded the same as a ball landing on clear ground. See also Rule 20(e).

RULE 24

Good Return

It is a good return:

(a) If the ball touch the net, posts, singles sticks, cord or metal cable, strap or band, provided that it passes over any of them and hits the ground within the Court; or

(b) If the ball, served or returned, hit the ground within the proper Court and rebound or be blown back over the net, and the player whose turn it is to strike reach over the net and play the ball, provided that neither he nor any part of his clothes or racket touch the net, posts, singles sticks, cord or metal cable, strap or band or the ground within his opponent's Court, and that the stroke be otherwise good; or

(c) If the ball be returned outside the post, or singles stick, either above or below the level of the top of the net, even though it touch the post or singles stick, provided that it hits the ground within the proper Court; or

(d) If a player's racket pass over the net after he has returned the ball, provided the ball pass the net before being played and be properly returned; or

(e) If a player succeeds in returning the ball, served or in play, which strikes a ball lying in the Court.

USTA Comment: *i.e., on his court when the point started; if the ball in play strikes a ball, rolling or stationary, that has come from elsewhere (other then from a player's hand or person; see 20(g) after the point started, a let should be called.*

Note: In a singles match, if, for the sake of convenience, a doubles Court be equipped with the singles sticks for the purpose of a singles game, then the doubles posts and those portions of the net, cord or metal cable and the band outside such singles sticks shall at all times be permanent fixtures, and are not regarded as posts or parts of the net of a singles game.

A return that passes under the net cord between the singles stick and adjacent doubles post without touching either net cord, net or doubles posts and falls within the area of play, is a good return.

USTA Comment: *But in doubles this would be a "through" — loss of point.*

Case 1. A ball going out of Court hits a net post or singles stick and falls within the lines of the opponent's Court. Is the stroke good?

Decision. If a service no, under Rule 10(c). If other than a service yes, under Rule 24(a).

Case 2. Is it a good return if a player returns the ball holding his racket in both hands?

Decision. Yes.

Case 3. The service, or ball in play, strikes a ball lying in the Court. Is the point won or lost thereby?

USTA Comment: *A ball that is touching a boundary line is considered to be "lying in the court".*

Decision. No. Play must continue. If it is not clear to the Umpire that the right ball is returned a let should be called.

Case 4. May a player use more than one racket at any time during play?

Decision. No; the whole implication of the Rules is singular.

Case 5. May a player request that a ball or balls lying in his opponent's Court be removed?

Decision. Yes, but not while a ball is in play.

USTA Comment: *The request must be honored.*

RULE 25

Interference

In case a player is hindered in making a stroke by anything not within his control, except a permanent fixture of the Court, or except as provided for in Rule 21, a let shall be called.

Case 1. A spectator gets into the way of a player, who fails to return the ball. May the player then claim a let?

Decision. Yes, if in the Umpire's opinion he was obstructed by circumstances beyond his control, but not if due to permanent fixtures of the Court or the arrangements of the ground.

Case 2. A player is interfered with as in Case No. 1, and the Umpire calls a let. The Server had previously served a fault. Has he the right to two services?

Decision. Yes: as the ball is in play, the point, not merely the stroke, must be replayed as the Rule provides.

Case 3. May a player claim a let under Rule 25 because he thought his opponent was being hindered, and consequently did not expect the ball to be returned?

Decision. No.

Case 4. Is a stroke good when a ball in play hits another ball in play?

Decision. A let should be called unless the other ball is in the air by the act of one of the players, in which case the Umpire will decide under Rule 21.

Case 5. If an Umpire or other judge erroneously calls "fault" or "out", and then corrects himself, which of the calls shall prevail?

Decision. A let must be called unless, in the opinion of the Umpire, neither player is hindered in his game, in which case the corrected call shall prevail.

Case 6. If the first ball served — a fault — rebounds, interfering with the Receiver at the time of the second service, may the Receiver claim a let?

Decision. Yes. But if he had an opportunity to remove the ball from the Court and negligently failed to do so, he may not claim a let.

Case 7. Is it a good stroke if the ball touches a stationary or moving object on the Court?

Decision. It is a good stroke unless the stationary object came into Court after the ball was put into play in which case a let must be called. If the ball in play strikes an object moving along or above the surface of the Court a let must be called.

Case 8. What is the ruling if the first service is a fault, the second service correct, and it becomes necessary to call a let either under the provision of Rule 25 or if the Umpire is unable to decide the point?

Decision. The fault shall be annulled and the whole point replayed.

USTA Comment: *See Rule 13 and Explanation thereto.*

RULE 26

The Game

If a player wins his first point, the score is called 15 for that player; on winning his second point, the score is called 30 for that player; on winning his third point, the score is called 40 for that player, and the fourth point won by a player is scored game for that player except as below:

If both players have won three points, the score is called deuce; and the next point won by a player is scored advantage for that player. If the same player win the next point, he wins the game; if the other player wins the next point the score is again called deuce; and so on, until a player wins the two points immediately following the score at deuce, when the game is scored for that player.

USTA Comment: *In matches played without an umpire the Server should announce, in a voice audible to his opponent and spectators, the set score at the beginning of each game, and (audible at least to his opponent) point scores as the game goes on. Misunderstandings will be avoided if this practice is followed.*

RULE 27

The Set and the Tie-Break System

(a) A player (or players) who first wins six games wins a set; except that he must win by a margin of two games over his opponent and where necessary a set shall be extended until this margin be achieved.

(b) The tie-break system of scoring may be adopted as an alternative to the advantage set system in paragraph (a) of this Rule provided the decision is announced in advance of the match.

In this case, the following Rules shall be effective:

The tie-break shall operate when the score reaches six games all in any set except in the third or fifth set of a three set or five set match respectively when an ordinary advantage set shall be played, unless otherwise decided and announced in advance of the match.

The following system shall be used in a tie-break game.

Singles

(i) A player who first wins seven points shall win the game and the set provided he leads by a margin of two points. If the score reaches six points all the game shall be extended until this margin has been achieved. Numerical scoring shall be used throughout the tie-break game.

(ii) The player whose turn it is to serve shall be the server for the first point. His opponent shall be the server for the second and third points and thereafter each player shall serve alternately for two consecutive points until the winner of the game and set has been decided.

(iii) From the first point, each service shall be delivered alternately from the right and left courts, beginning from the right court. If service from a wrong half of the court occurs and is undetected, all play resulting from such wrong service or services shall stand, but the inaccuracy of station shall be corrected immediately it is discovered.

(iv) Players shall change ends after every six points and at the conclusion of the tie-break game.

(v) The tie-break game shall count as one game for the ball change, except that, if the balls are due to be changed at the beginning of the tie-break, the change shall be delayed until the second game of the following set.

Doubles

In doubles the procedure for singles shall apply. The player whose turn it is to serve shall be the server for the first point. Thereafter each player shall serve in rotation for two points, in the same order as previously in that set, until the winners of the game and set have been decided.

Rotation of Service

The player (or pair in the case of doubles) who served first in the tie-break game shall receive service in the first game of the following set.

Case 1. The tie-break is played, although it has been decided and announced in advance of the match that an advantage set will be played. Are the points already played counted?

Decision. If the error is discovered before a point has been completed, a let shall be played and the game re-started.

If a point has been completed, the tie-break scoring system shall continue to operate until the game is won, and that game shall be regarded as the final game of the set.

If the game has been completed, the result of the set shall stand.

Case 2. If during the tie-break in a doubles game a partner receives out of turn, or a player serves out of

rotation, shall the order of receiving, or serving as the case may be, remain as altered until the end of the game?

Decision. Yes.

RULE 28

Maximum Number of Sets

The maximum number of sets in a match shall be 5, or, where women take part, 3.

RULE 29

Rules Apply to Both Sexes

Except where otherwise stated, every reference in these Rules to the masculine includes the feminine gender.

RULE 30

Decisions of Umpire and Referee

In matches where an Umpire is appointed, his decision shall be final; but where a Referee is appointed, an appeal shall lie to him from the decision of an Umpire on a question of law, and in all such cases the decision of the Referee shall be final.

In matches where assistants to the Umpire are appointed (Linesmen, Net-cord Judges, Foot-fault Judges) their decisions shall be final on questions of fact except that if in the opinion of an Umpire a clear mistake has been made he shall have the right to change the decision of an assistant or order a let to be played. When such an assistant is unable to give a decision he shall indicate this immediately to the Umpire who shall give a decision. When an Umpire is unable to give a decision on a question of fact he shall order a let to be played.

In Davis Cup matches or other team competitions where a Referee·is on Court, any decision can be changed by the Referee, who may also instruct an Umpire to order a let to be played.

The Referee, in his discretion, may at any time postpone a match on account of darkness or the condition of the ground or the weather. In any case of postponement the previous score and previous occupancy of Courts shall hold good, unless the Referee and the players unanimously agree otherwise.

Case 1. The Umpire orders a let, but a player claims that the point should not be replayed. May the Referee be requested to give a decision?

Decision. Yes. A question of tennis law, that is an issue relating to the application of specific facts, shall first be determined by the Umpire. However, if the Umpire is uncertain or if a player appeals from his determination, then the Referee shall be requested to give a Decision, and his decision is final.

Case 2. A ball is called out, but a player claims that the ball was good. May the Referee give a ruling?

Decision. No. This is a question of fact, that is an issue relating to what actually occurred during a specific incident, and the decision of the on-court officials is therefore final.

Case 3. May an Umpire overrule a Linesman at the end of a rally if, in his opinion, a clear mistake has been made during the course of a rally?

Decision. No, unless in his opinion the opponent was hindered. Otherwise an Umpire may only overrule a Linesman if he does so immediately after the mistake has been made.

Case 4. A Linesman calls a ball out. The Umpire was unable to see clearly, although he thought the ball was in. May he overrule the Linesman?

Decision. No. An Umpire may only overrule if he considers that a call was incorrect beyond all reasonable doubt. He may only overrule a ball determined good by a Linesman if he has been able to see a space between the ball and the line; and he may only overrule a ball determined out, or a fault, by a Linesman if he has seen the ball hit the line, or fall inside the line.

Case 5. May a Linesman change his call after the Umpire has given the score?

Decision. No. If a Linesman realises he has made an error, he must call "correction" immediately so that the Umpire and players are aware of his error before the score is given.

Case 6. A player claims his return shot was good after a Linesman called "out". May the Umpire overrule the Linesman?

Decision. No. An Umpire may never overrule as a result of a protest or an appeal by a player.

USTA Comment: *See Rule 17, Case 1.*

RULE 31

Continuous Play and Rest Periods

Play shall be continuous from the first service till the match be concluded.

(a) Notwithstanding the above, after the third set, or when women take part the second set, either player is entitled to a rest, which shall not exceed 10 minutes, or in countries situated between Latitude 15 degrees North and Latitude 15 degrees South, 45 minutes and furthermore, when necessitated by circumstances not within the control of the players, the Umpire may suspend play for such a period as he may consider necessary.

If play be suspended and be not resumed until a later day the rest may be taken only after the third set (or when women take part the second set) of play on such later day, completion of an unfinished set being counted as one set.

If play be suspended and not resumed until 10 minutes have elapsed in the same day the rest may be taken only after three consecutive sets have been played without interruption (or when women take part two sets), completion of an unfinished set being counted as one set.

Any nation and/or committee organising a tournament, match or competition, other than the International Tennis Championships (Davis Cup and Federation Cup), is at liberty to modify this provision or omit it from its regulations provided this is announced before play commences.

USTA Rules Regarding Rest Periods

Regular MEN's and WOMEN's, and MEN's and WOMEN's Amateur — Paragraph (a) of Rule 31 applies, except that a tournament using tie-breaks may eliminate rest periods provided advance notice is given.

BOYS' 18 — All matches in this division shall be best of three sets with NO REST PERIOD, except that in interscholastic, state, sectional and national championships the FINAL ROUND may be best-of-five sets. If such a final requires more than three sets to decide it, a rest of 10 minutes after the third set is mandatory. Special Note: In severe temperature-humidity conditions the Referee may rule that a 10-minute rest may be taken in a Boys' 18 best-of-three before the third set. However, to be valid this must be done before the match is started, and as a matter of the Referee's independent judgment.

BOYS' 16, 14 and 12, and GIRLS' 18, 16, 14 and 12 — All matches in these categories shall be best of three sets. A 10-minute rest before the third set is MANDATORY in Girls' 12, 14 and 16, and BOYS' 12 and 14. The rest period is OPTIONAL in GIRLS' 18 and BOYS' 16. (Optional means at the option of any competitor.)

All SENIOR divisions (35 and over), Mother-Daughter, Father-Son and similar combinations: Under conventional scoring, all matches best of three sets, with rest period at any player's option.

When 'NO-AD' scoring is used in a tournament the committee may stipulate that there will be no rest periods. Two conditions of this stipulation are: (1) Advance notice must be given on entry blanks for the event, and (2) The Referee is empowered to reinstate the normal rest periods for matches played under unusually severe temperature-humidity conditions; to be valid, such reinstatement must be announced before a given match or series of matches is started, and be a matter of the Referee's independent judgment.

USTA Comment: *When a player competes in an event designated as for players of a bracket whose rules as to intermissions and length of match are geared to a different physical status, the player cannot ask for allowances based on his or her age, or her sex.*

For example, a female competing in an inter-collegiate (men's) varsity team match would not be entitled to claim a rest period in a best-of-three-sets match unless that were the condition under which the team competition was normally held.

(b) Play shall never be suspended, delayed or interfered with for the purpose of enabling a player to recover his strength or his breath.

(c) A maximum of 30 seconds shall elapse from the moment the ball goes out of play at the end of one point to the time the ball is struck for the next point, except that when changing ends a maximum of one minute thirty seconds shall elapse from the moment the ball goes out of play at the end of the game to the time the ball is struck for the first point of the next game.

The Umpire shall use his discretion when there is interference which makes it impossible for the server to serve within that time.

These provisions shall be strictly construed. The Umpire shall be the sole judge of any suspension, delay or interference, and after giving due warning he may disqualify the offender.

Note: A Tournament Committee has discretion to decide the time allowed for a warm-up period prior to a match. It is recommended that this does not exceed five minutes.

Case 1. A player's clothing, footwear, or equipment (excluding racket) becomes out of adjustment in such a way that it is impossible or undesirable for him to play on. May play be suspended while the maladjustment is rectified?

Decision: If this occurs in circumstances outside the control of the player, a suspension may be allowed. The Umpire shall be the judge of whether a suspension is justified and the period of the suspension.

Case 2. If, owing to an accident, a player is unable to continue immediately, is there any limit to the time during which play may be suspended?

Decision. No allowance may be made for natural loss of physical condition. In the case of accidental injury the Umpire may allow a one-time, three minute suspension for that injury. Play must resume in three minutes. However, the organizers of international circuits and team events recognized by the ITF may extend this if treatment is necessary.

USTA Comment: *Case 2 refers to an important distinction that should be made between a disability caused by an accident during the match, and disability attributable to fatigue, illness or exertion (examples: cramps, muscle pull, vertigo, strained back). Accidental loss embodies a sprained ankle or actual injury from such mishaps as collision with netpost or net, a cut from a fall, contact with chair or backstop, or being hit with a ball, racket or other object. An injured player shall not be permitted to leave the playing area. If, in the*

opinion of the Umpire, there is a genuine toilet emergency, a bona fide toilet visit by a player is permissible and is not to be considered natural loss of condition.

Case 3. During a doubles game, may one of the partners leave the Court while the ball is in play?

Decision. Yes, so long as the Umpire is satisfied that play is continuous within the meaning of the Rules, and that there is no conflict with Rules 36 and 37.

USTA Comment: *When a match is resumed following an interruption necessitated by weather conditions, it is allowable for the players to engage in a "re-warm-up" period. It may be of the same duration as the warm-up allowed at the start of the match; may be done using the balls that were in play at the time of the interruption, and the time for the next ball change shall not be affected by this.*

RULE 32

Coaching

During the playing of a match in a team competition, a player may receive coaching from a captain who is sitting on the court only when he changes ends at the end of a game, but not when he changes ends during a tie-break game.

A player may not receive coaching during the playing of any other match.

The provisions of this rule must be strictly construed. After due warning an offending player may be disqualified.

Case 1. Should a warning be given, or the player be disqualified, if the coaching is given by signals in an unobtrusive manner?

Decision. The Umpire must take action as soon as he becomes aware that coaching is being given verbally or by signals. If the Umpire is unaware that coaching is being given, a player may draw his attention to the fact that advice is being given.

Case 2. Can a player receive coaching during the ten minute rest in a five set match, or when play is interrupted and he leaves the court?

Decision. Yes. In these circumstances, when the player is not on the court, there is no restriction on coaching.

Note: The word "coaching" includes any advice or instruction.

RULE 33

Ball Change Error

In cases where balls are changed after an agreed number of games, if the balls are not changed in the correct sequence the mistake shall be corrected when the player, or pair in the case of doubles, who should have served with the new balls is next due to serve.

THE DOUBLES GAME

RULE 34

The above Rules shall apply to the Doubles Game except as below.

RULE 35

Dimensions of Court

For the Doubles Game, the Court shall be 36 feet (10.97m.) in width, i.e. 4½ feet (1.37m.) wider on each side than the Court for the Singles Game, and those portions of the singles side-lines which lie between the two service-lines shall be called the service side-lines. In other respects, the Court shall be similar to that described in Rule 1, but the portions of the singles side-lines between the base-line and service-line on each side of the net may be omitted if desired.

USTA Case 1. In doubles the Server claims the right to stand at the corner of the court as marked by the doubles sideline. Is the foregoing correct or is it necessary that the Server stand within the limits of the center mark and the singles sideline?

Decision. The Server has the right to stand anywhere back of the baseline between the center mark extension and the doubles sideline extension.

RULE 36

Order of Service

The order of serving shall be decided at the beginning of each set as follows:

The pair who have to serve in the first game of each set shall decide which partner shall do so and the opposing pair shall decide similarly for the second game. The partner of the player who served in the first game shall serve in the third; the partner of the player who served in the second game shall serve in the fourth, and so on in the same order in all the subsequent games of a set.

Case 1. In doubles, one player does not appear in time to play, and his partner claims to be allowed to play single-handed against the opposing players. May he do so?

Decision. No.

RULE 37

Order of Receiving

The order of receiving the service shall be decided at the beginning of each set as follows:

The pair who have to receive the service in the first game shall decide which partner shall receive the first service, and that partner shall continue to receive the first service in every odd game throughout that set. The opposing pair shall likewise decide which partner shall receive the first service in the

second game and that partner shall continue to receive the first service in every even game throughout that set. Partners shall receive the service alternately throughout each game.

Case 1. Is it allowable in doubles for the Server's partner to stand in a position that obstructs the view of the Receiver?

Decision. Yes. The Server's partner may take any position on his side of the net in or out of the Court that he wishes.

USTA Comment: *The same is true of the Receiver's partner.*

RULE 38

Service Out of Turn

If a partner serve out of his turn, the partner who ought to have served shall serve as soon as the mistake is discovered, but all points scored, and any faults served before such discovery, shall be reckoned. If a game shall have been completed before such discovery, the order of service remains as altered.

USTA Comment: *For an exception to Rule 38 see Case 2 under Rule 27.*

RULE 39

Error in Order of Receiving

If during a game the order of receiving the service is changed by the Receivers it shall remain as altered until the end of the game in which the mistake is discovered, but the partners shall resume their original order of receiving in the next game of that set in which they are Receivers of the service.

RULE 40

Ball Touching Server's Partner Is Fault

The service is a fault as provided for by Rule 10, or if the ball touch the Server's partner or anything which he wears or carries; but if the ball served touch the partner of the Receiver, or anything which he wears or carries, not being a let under Rule 14(a) before it hits the ground, the Server wins the point.

RULE 41

Ball Struck Alternately

The ball shall be struck alternately by one or other player of the opposing pairs, and if a player touches the ball in play with his racket in contravention of this Rule, his opponents win the point.

USTA Comment: *This means that, in the course of making one return, only one member* of a doubles team may hit the ball. If both of them hit the ball, either simultaneously or consecutively, it is an illegal return. The partners themselves do not have to "alternate" in making returns. Mere clashing of rackets does not make a return illegal, if it is clear that only one racket touched the ball.

If you have a rules problem, send full details, enclosing a stamped self-addressed envelope, to Nick Powel, USTA Tennis Rules Committee, 3147 South 14th Street, Arlington, Virginia, 22204, and you will be sent a prompt explanation.

APPENDIX

Regulations for Making Tests Specified in Rule 3

1. Unless otherwise specified all tests shall be made at a temperature of approximately 68° Fahrenheit (20° Centigrade) and a relative humidity of approximately 60 per cent. All balls should be removed from their container and kept at the recognized temperature and humidity for 24 hours prior to testing, and shall be at that temperature and humidity when the test is commenced.

2. Unless otherwise specified the limits are for a test conducted in an atmospheric pressure resulting in a barometric reading of approximately 30 inches (76cm.).

3. Other standards may be fixed for localities where the average temperature, humidity or average barometric pressure at which the game is being played differ materially from 68° Fahrenheit (20° Centigrade), 60 per cent and 30 inches (76cm.) respectively.
Applications for such adjusted standards may be made by any National Association to the International Tennis Federation and if approved shall be adopted for such localities.

4. In all tests for diameter a ring gauge shall be used consisting of a metal plate, preferably non-corrosive, of a uniform thickness of one-eighth of an inch (.32cm.) in which there are two circular openings 2,575 inches (6.54cm.) and 2,700 inches (6.86cm.) in diameter respectively. The inner surface of the gauge shall have a convex profile with a radius of one-sixteenth of an inch (.16cm.). The ball shall not drop through the smaller opening by its own weight and shall drop through the larger opening by its own weight.

5. In all tests for deformation conducted under Rule 3, the machine designed by Percy Herbert Stevens and patented in Great Britain under Patent No. 230250, together with the subsequent additions and improvements thereto, including the modi-

fications required to take return deformations, shall be employed or such other machine which is approved by a National Association and gives equivalent readings to the Stevens machine.

6. Procedure for carrying out tests.
(a) Pre-compression. Before any ball is tested it shall be steadily compressed by approximately one inch (2.51cm.) on each of the three diameters at right angles to one another in succession; this process to be carried out three times (nine compressions in all). All tests to be completed within two hours of precompression.
(b) Bound test (as in Rule 3). Measurements are to be taken from the concrete base to the bottom of the ball.
(c) Size test (as in paragraph 1 above).
(d) Weight test (as in Rule 3).
(e) Deformation test. The ball is placed in position on the modified Stevens machine so that neither platen of the machine is in contact with the cover seam. The contact weight is applied, the pointer and the mark brought level, and the dials set to zero. The test weight equivalent to 18lb. (8.165kg.) is placed on the beam and pressure applied by turning the wheel at a uniform speed so that five seconds elapse from the instant the beam leaves its seat until the pointer is brought level with the mark. When turning ceases the reading is recorded (forward deformation). The wheel is turned again until figure ten is reached on the scale (one inch [2.5cm.] deformation). The wheel is then rotated in the opposite direction at a uniform speed (thus releasing pressure) until the beam pointer again coincides with the mark. After waiting ten seconds the pointer is adjusted to the mark if necessary. The reading is then recorded (return deformation). This procedure is repeated on each ball across the two diameters at right angles to the initial position and to each other.

INDEX

A

Achilles' tendon, 92, 96
action for balls in flight, 7
action of ball striking the court surface
  underspin, 7
  sidespin, 7
  topspin, 7
advent of television, (2) ch 16
American twist serve, 85
angled overhead smash, 85
anxiety, 152
approach shots, 8, 40, 141
attacking
  beating the net player, 116
  change of pace tactics, 117
  closing in on the net, 115
  division line theory, 110, 114
  going to the net following serve, 114
  going to the net following an approach
    shot, 114
  going to the net off a
    groundstroke, 115
  overhead smashes, 119
  passing shots to beat a net player, 116
  strategy to beat a player who attacks
    the net, 116
Australian doubles, 128

B

backhand groundstroke, 9
backhand overhead smash, 72
backhand volley, 44
ballistic stretch, 93
basic backhand
  contact, 25
  follow through, 25
  footwork, weight transfer, and leg
    power, 25
  grip, 24
  preparation, 24
  racket control, 25
  wrist, elbow, shoulder position, 25
basic flat serve
  contact from the half serve position, 53
  execution of full versus half serve
    position, 54
  grip, 51
  service stance, 51

toss,
  holding the ball for the, 51
  how to toss the ball, 51
  synchronization as preparation for
    the serve, 52
basic forehand
  contact with the ball, 14
  follow through, 15
  footwork and early preparation, 6
  grip, 13
  loop, 14
  preparation, 14
  position of the elbow and wrist, and
    the transfer of weight, 15
behavior on a tennis court
  appropriate clothing, 99
  ball is in play, 100
  being a partner in warm-up, 99
  emotion, 100
  how to return tennis balls, 100
  how to request tennis balls, 100
  talking on a tennis court, 99
  walking on to a tennis court, 99
  when a ball is called out on a line call,
    100
blisters, 95
bruising, 95
bouncing the overhead, 71

C

changing
  grip, 24
  side of court, 103
choice of serve, side of court, and order
  of service, 102
chop, 83
combining serve and volley, 144
communications, 130
competition
  anger and losing temper, 151
  anxiety and slumps, 152
  concentration, 151
  execution over winning, 150
  fear of
    losing, 151
    winning, 151
  flow, 152
  negative attitudes or feelings, 150
  "psyching out", 151

relaxation
  contribution of, 153
  pre-match, 154
  progressive, 154
  tension on the court, 153
concentration, 151
conditioning, 97
contact with the ball, 15, 18, 25, 29, 31,
  35, 44
continental grip
  backhand groundstroke, 2
  backhand volley, 44
  forehand groundstroke, 2
  forehand volley, 43
conventional doubles, 125
cramps, 95
cross court, 142

D

differences between
  backhand basic flat groundstroke and
    slice backhand groundstoke, 32
  backhand basic flat groundstroke and
    topspin backhand groundstroke, 30
  backhand basic flat groundstroke and
    two-hand backhand groundstroke, 35
  forehand basic flat groundstroke and
    slice forehand groundstroke, 21
  forehand basic flat groundstroke and
    topspin forehand groundstroke, 19
dink shots, 84
division
  line theory, 114, 129, 135
  of court, 110
  theory of play, 112
drills
  approach, 139
  baseline, 142
  bounce hit, 143
  combination down the line and cross
    court, 142
  combination groundstroke and
    volley, 145
  concentration, 143
  cross court, 142
  down the sideline, 142
  grooving, 140
  groundstroke, 138
  groundstroke, volley, lob,
    overhead, 145
  lob, overhead, 146
  moving, 140
  overhead, 141
  serve and return, 143
  serve and volley, 144
  serving, 137
  twenty-one, 143
  working up volley, 145
dropping and hitting the ball, 37
drop shots and volleys, 84
dump shots, 84, 85

E

eastern
  backhand grip, 2
  forehand grip, 1
economics, (3) ch 16
execution over winning, 150
eye-hand coordination, 9

F

fault, 106
fear of,
  losing, 151
  winning, 151
feel and timing of the ball, 9
flat racket face, 6
flat serve, 9
flow, 152
focus, 10, 12
foot fault, 106
forehand basic flat groundstroke, 8, 15
forehand slice groundstroke, 21
forehand topspin groundstroke, 17
forehand volley, 43
foundation, 39

G

going to the net,
  closing in on the net, 115
  following an approach shot, 114
  following serve, 114
  off a groundstroke, 115
grips,
  continental backhand, 2
  continental forehand, 2
  eastern backhand, 2
  eastern forehand, 1
  two-hand backhand, 4
  western forehand, 3
groundstrokes,
  approach, 9, 40
  basic flat backhand, 8, 14
  basic flat forehand, 8, 13
  slice backhand, 9, 31
  slice forehand, 9, 21
  topspin backhand, 9, 28
  topspin forehand, 9, 17
  two-hand backhand, 34

H

haematoma, 95
half volleys, 9, 82
hand signals, 130
high volley, 48
homebase, 38
how to react and get to the ball, 88

I

incorporation of the,
  lob in the total game, 79
  overhead smash in the total game, 72
  volley in the total game, 49

injuries,
    common tennis, 95
    treatment of, 96

L

let, 105
lob,
    defensive lob with the racket in the
        up position, 77
    defensive lob with underspin, 76
    defensive lob in the total game, 73
    defensive lob with modest topspin, 75
    flight patterns, 74
    moonball, 74
    offensive lob, 75
    racket control, weight transfer, &
        movement of the feet, 78
    strategy, 135
    topspin lob, 75
    volley, 85
location of players during serve and
    receiving, 103
low volley, 48

M

mental
    imagery, 154
    rehearsal, 154
mixed doubles, 127
moonball, 74
moving to the ball, 38

N

net play,
    air game, 134
    receiver of serve, 135
    receiver's partner, 135
    serves, 133
    serving partner, 133
    serving team, 133
nutrition,
    as related to a match, 98
    before the match, 98
    during the match, 98
    following the match, 98
    taking care of yourself, 95
    weight and diet for tennis, 97

O

one up-one back formation, 124
one word communication, 130
open racket face, 6
open stance, 88
order of serve, 103
overhead smash,
    advancing to more agility, 70
    air game, 136
    backhand, 72
    basic, 9
    bouncing the, 71
    jump overhead smash, 70

orthodox, 69
scissors, kick, 70
strategy, 135

P

partners, which serves first, 130
percentage tennis, 109
physical conditioning, 97
pick up manuever,
    ball bounce, 82
    lifting action, 81
placing the ball in play, 105
poach, 125
punch action, 6
pulled muscle, 95

R

racket control,
    basic swing action, 6
    punch action, 6
    throwing action, 6
racket face,
    closed, 6
    flat, 6
    open, 6
ready position,
    basic, 10
    serve, 51
    volley, 43
relaxation,
    pre-match, 154
    progressive, 154
restringing of rackets, 164
return of serve,
    anticipation, 66
    consideration of spin and velocity, 65
    effectively, 65
    in doubles, 132
    ready position, 65
    strategy, 112
    target, 66

S

serves,
    as part of strategy, 111
    full versus half serve, 54
    grip for flat service, 51
    half service position, 53
    slice, 57
    slice differs from the flat serve, 57
    topspin, 9, 60
    toss, 51
    toss synchronization, 52
scoring a game, set, match, 104
selecting string, 160
signals, 132
slice groundstroke,
    backhand,
        contact, 31
        follow through, 31
        grip, 31

preparation, 31
forehand
  contact, 21
  follow through, 22
  grip, 21
  preparation, 21
slump, 152
social doubles, 123
spins,
  action of the ball striking the court
  surface,
    underspin, 7
    sidespin, 7
    topspin, 7
  basic action for balls in flight, 7
  comprehending, 7
  sidespin, 7
  slice, 9
  topspin, 7
  underspin, 7
sprained ankle, 95
stepping into the ball, 88
strategy,
  attacking the net, 113, 133
  baseline play, 120
  beat the player attacking the net, 116
  doubles, 123
  lob & overhead, 117, 135
  overall game strategy & plan, 121, 136
  percentage tennis, 109
  scoring situations, 121
  serves, 111, 131
static stretch, 91
stretching, 91

T

tennis,
  ball selection, 161
  clothing, 161
  court dimensions, 102
  court surfaces, 157
  elbow, 96
  professionals, 168
  tournaments, 163
throwing action, 6
tie breakers, 104
timing, 89
timing & feel for the ball, 9, 83
topspin groundstrokes,
  backhand,
    contact, 29
    follow through, 29
    grip, 29
    preparation, 29
  change of grip, 18
  forehand,
    contact, 18
    follow through, 19
    grip, 18
    preparation, 18

topspin serve,
  basic, 9, 60
  difference from the flat serve, 60,
    61, 62
two-hand backhand,
  contact, 35
  follow through, 35
  grip, 34
  preparation, 34

U

USTA National Rating Program, 164
USTA, 166

V

volley,
  anticipation, 46
  ball hit at the player, 48
  basic, 9
  contact, 44
  follow through, 44
  footwork, 46
  grip, 43
  half volley, 9, 82
  high volley, 48
  lob volley, 85
  low volley, 48
  ready position, 43
  set up, 47
  wide ball, 43

W

warm-down, 94
warm-up, 94
western grip, 3
when to advance to the next level of
  groundstroke skill, 41
who plays where and when, 128
who plays which side of the court on
  return of serve, 128